They're Still Here

They're Still Here: A Medium Shares the Proof That Love Never Dies

True Stories of Connection, Healing and the Presence of Spirit

By

Sharon Valenti

A Perfect Soul Publishing

Canton, GA

Published by **A Perfect Soul Publishing**

Canton, GA

ISBN (Paperback): 979-8-9940611-1-4

ISBN (Hardcover): 979-8-9940611-2-1

ISBN (eBook): 979-8-9940611-0-7

Library of Congress Control Number: 2025925322

Printed in the United States of America
10 9 8 7 6 5 4 3 2 1

Dedicated to my son, Shah Hashemi.

Your love, your light, and your presence continue to guide me every single day.

Acknowledgments

My deepest gratitude goes to Kevin Mansoor, Amazon bestselling author of The Trinitarian Knight Collection, whose encouragement gave me the final push to begin this book and whose guidance helped me shape it with clarity and purpose. I am equally thankful for the support of Kristen Williams, Jose Burgos, and Cassandra Manheimer. Their time, kindness, and steady presence throughout this journey meant more than they know. Each of you has played a meaningful role, and I am truly grateful.

To my husband, Frank, thank you for allowing me the uninterrupted time I needed to complete this manuscript.

TABLE OF CONTENTS

CHAPTER 1

What is Mediumship?

CHAPTER   2

The Spirit World–

A Glimpse Beyond the Veil

CHAPTER   3

The Mechanics of Communication–

How It Works

CHAPTER 4

Finding a Reputable Medium

CHAPTER 5

Opening the Door Within

CHAPTER 6

Grief as a Sacred Invitation

CHAPTER 7

Soul Contracts, Life Purpose & Why Some Deaths Feel "Too Soon"

CHAPTER 8

Children and Spirit Communication

CHAPTER 9

Your Personal Pathway to Spirit

CHAPTER 10

Living a Spiritually Connected Life

Quick Reference Guide

Glossary of Spiritual Terms

Preface

This book is for anyone who has ever loved, lost, and whispered a question into the empty air: "Are you still there?"

It was born from the moment my world shattered, the sudden passing of my beloved son, Shah. It is the story of how my deepest, most devastating grief became an unexpected doorway to a love that does not die, a connection that transcends the veil we call death.

This is more than my story. It is a guide on your own journey. A way to quiet the fear, recognize the whispers, and discover the profound comfort of knowing that the bonds of the soul are forever. Turn the page, and let's begin.

Author's Note

Dear Reader,

There are moments in life that divide everything into a before and an after. For me, that moment was the day my beloved son, Shah, left this world. His passing was sudden, unexpected, and devastating in ways I still struggle to put into words. In an instant, the world I knew collapsed, and I stood in the emptiness, lost and hollowed out by grief.

In those early days, I felt as if I were moving through a fog. I was in shock, so deep and consuming I didn't fully register my pain. Instead, I focused on caring for everyone else. I tried to be strong for my family, for my friends, for anyone who was mourning Shah. I set aside my sadness, thinking that if I kept going, I would be okay. And so I went on, day after day, on autopilot. Smiling when expected, speaking when spoken to, but inside, I was crumbling.

The first three months were the darkest of my life. I fell into a depression so deep that even getting out of bed felt impossible. I recall taking long walks where I would cry openly and ask for answers. I'd drive in my car, screaming at the top of my lungs until my throat was raw, or I'd find myself parked somewhere, with no memory of how I got there. The grief was all consuming. It swallowed time, memory, and light.

My body bore the shock too. I discovered my usually normal thyroid levels had skyrocketed, my system completely overwhelmed by the trauma. I began thyroid medication and an antidepressant, knowing I needed support in every form to keep going. And slowly, with help, I looked for a way through the darkness.

It was during those long, empty hours of grief that the seed of my sojourn into mediumship was planted. It wasn't my intention to become a medium. I was simply desperate to stay connected with my son. I began searching for ways to bridge the chasm between us. That search led me to take mediumship classes and training, first as a way to reach for Shah, and later, to my amazement, as a discovery I could commune not only with him, but with the dear ones of others.

What began as a desire to hold on to my little boy (even though he was a grown man at the time of his passing) became a calling to bring hope, comfort, and healing to those, like me, who have stood in the wreckage of loss. I did not choose this path. It chose me, through my deepest heartbreak, my greatest love, and my need to understand that even in the darkest night, the bonds of the soul endure.

I offer this book from that place in my heart. My hope is the pages ahead will help you experience less alone, remind you that your rapport with those in the afterlife continues, and give you tools to navigate the profound, often painful, and always transformative passage of grief and spirit connection.

With Love,

Sharon

CHAPTER 1

What is Mediumship?

Flickering candlelight casts long shadows across a velvet-draped table. A group of strangers holds hands, their faces a mixture of fear and hushed anticipation. At the head of the table sits a figure, eyes closed, who suddenly speaks in a deep, sepulchral voice, delivering a cryptic message from a world beyond our own.

This is the scene Hollywood has painted for us a thousand times. It's the image that often springs to mind when we hear the word medium, a dramatic, spooky affair, steeped in mystery and theatricality. While it makes for great cinema, it has very little to do with the profound and mending experience genuine mediumship can be.

The reality for most people today is far less theatrical and infinitely more meaningful. Picture this instead: a quiet room, perhaps with sunlight streaming through a window. You are sitting comfortably in a chair, opposite a warm and ordinary person who speaks in a normal, conversational tone. There are no special effects, no ghostly apparitions. There is simply a conversation, a three-way call between you, the medium, and a dear one who has passed from this life but whose consciousness, personality, and affection for you endure. What would it mean to you to know, beyond doubt, that someone you've lost is still right beside you?

Mediumship is not just an ability; it is a hallowed truth. It is the art and practice of mediating communication between human beings and those who have transitioned into the afterlife world. A genuine medium does not guess or make vague statements. They act as the bridge between this world and the next, offering undeniable evidence, heartfelt linking, and life-altering confirmation of what is already written in your soul: that life, connection, and consciousness never end. This truth is foundational to everything you'll read in this book. We'll explore not only how mediumship works, but why it matters so deeply to so many.

The Three Pillars of a Reading

To truly understand how a reading works, it's helpful to think of it as a delicate partnership supported by three essential pillars. A successful and comforting relationship relies on the presence and cooperation of all three. If one pillar is weak, the entire bridge can feel unstable. These three pillars are: the medium, the sitter, and the spirit communicator.

1. The Medium

Mediums are the most visible pillar, but their job is not to be the star of the show. Their role is to be a clear and passive instrument. An excellent medium has spent years training to quiet their own mind, ego, and beliefs to become a receptive channel for communing. They are not summoning or controlling the realm of souls; they are simply making themselves available, creating an energetic invitation for those in the unseen realm to draw close and speak through them. Their primary responsibility is to relay the information they receive with integrity and without interpretation.

2. The Sitter

You are the second equally important pillar. You are the reason for the bond, the anchor in the physical world the spirit communicator is trying to reach.

3. The Spirit Communicator

The third pillar is the one on the other side of the veil: your loved one in the energetic plane. They are not a vague, ethereal mist, but an intelligent consciousness with the same personality, memories, and caring they had in life. It takes a significant amount of effort for them to lower their vibration and impress their thoughts and feelings upon the medium's mind. They are just as invested in the reading's success as you are. They choose what evidence to share, a funny memory, a description of their passing, a mention of a recent family event they "observed", to prove to you it is truly them. Their goal is to offer you peace, solace, and the undeniable assurance of their continued existence.

Have you ever felt a presence in the room, one that brought comfort rather than fear? What if that was more than just a feeling?

Debunking Common Myths

Myth #1: Mediums talk to "stuck" or "trapped" ghosts.

The Reality: This is perhaps the biggest and most persistent myth. The goal of mediumship is not to contact troubled spirits lingering on the earthly plane. Instead, a medium establishes a link with souls who have fully and peacefully transitioned into the light of the energetic plane. The very purpose of their communication is to show you they are not stuck, lost, or in distress, but are vibrant, at peace, and still very much a part of your life. A reading is a reunion, not a rescue mission.

Myth #2: It's always spooky and frightening.

The Reality: While Hollywood adores associating spirit communication with fear, legitimate mediumship is rooted in the highest of all vibrations: love. The entire process is driven by the affection between you and those who have transitioned. The intention is always to bring comfort, validation, and a sense of wholeness, never fear. A reputable medium will ensure the energetic space is safe, protected, and positive. The feelings that come through most powerfully in a reading are almost always overwhelming caring, joy, and a profound sense of peace.

Why do we fear what we don't understand, especially when love may be the very thing knocking on the door?

Myth #3: A medium will tell you your future or solve all your problems.

The Reality: This myth confuses mediumship with fortune-telling. The primary purpose of a medium is to provide evidence of survival after death, proving your dearest ones are still with you. While the afterlife individual may offer a higher perspective or words of encouragement about your life path, they will not give you winning lottery numbers or make your life decisions for you. They respect your free will and your soul's path, which includes navigating your own challenges. A reading offers comfort for the past and present; it does not predict the future.

Myth #4: Mediums know everything about you.

The Reality: A medium is not an all-knowing mind reader. They are simply the go-between, the telephone operator establishing a link. They can only relay the information that the consciousness beyond chooses to share, and that information is almost always for validating their identity and bringing a message of comfort and caring to you, the sitter. The medium's access is limited. They will not know your bank account password or your deepest, darkest secrets unless it is information the spirit communicator feels is essential to share for the sake of mending and evidence. Your privacy is respected by both the medium and those in the afterlife.

A Brief History of Connecting Worlds

Throughout this chapter, and this book, you'll notice brief stories and case studies woven into the text. These real-life examples are not here to dramatize, but to humanize. They help bring abstract ideas and historical moments to life. By sharing the experiences of people who have walked this path before you, whether a grieving parent, a skeptical scholar, or a curious seeker, you'll gain a more personal, grounded understanding of mediumship and its emotional depth. My goal is not just to teach you what mediumship is, but to help you feel it.

Ancient Roots: The Desire for Connection Is Timeless

The desire to commune with those who have passed from the physical world is not a modern invention or a passing trend. It is a deeply ingrained, timeless human impulse that stretches back to the dawn of consciousness. Long before the first séance table was draped in velvet, cultures all across the globe sought wisdom, guidance, and comfort from the spirit world. While the names and methods have changed over millennia, the fundamental practice of bridging worlds has remained a constant.

Can you imagine a world so hungry for connection that a simple knock on a wall became a national obsession?

The Birth of Modern Spiritualism

While the practice of afterlife communication is ancient, the movement known as Modern Spiritualism has a very specific and dramatic beginning fueled by the widespread grief following the Civil War and a deep societal need for reassurance that unconditional affection ones were okay. It exploded into Western culture from a small, humble cabin in Hydesville, New York, in 1848. There, two young sisters, Maggie and Kate Fox, began hearing mysterious rapping and knocking sounds in their home. This ignited a cultural phenomenon that brought the concept of direct communication with those who had transitioned out of the shadows and into the very center of popular culture.

The Age of Investigation

The explosion of Spiritualism in the late 19th and early 20th centuries created a need to separate fact from fiction. This gave rise to the Age of Investigation, led by groups like the Society for Psychical Research (SPR), founded in 1882. Scholars and scientists applied rigorous methods to study mediumistic claims, shifting the focus from dramatic physical phenomena to the more subtle and verifiable art of mental mediumship—the receiving of specific, factual information that could be documented and studied.

Mediumship Today: A Return to Healing

After a period of quiet consolidation, mediumship has experienced a remarkable resurgence. The mediumship of today, however, is focused overwhelmingly on providing solace. Reputable mediums see themselves as grief support specialists, using evidential information to provide a safe space where people can process loss and receive the comforting assurance that their dearest ones are still present in their lives. This modern practice, built on a strong code of ethics, has transformed mediumship into a legitimate and powerful tool for those navigating the universal human experience of loss.

Isn't it comforting to know that something as ancient as spirit communication can still meet us in our modern grief?

Mediumship vs. Psychic Abilities: A Crucial Distinction

The Golden Rule: "All mediums are psychic, but not all psychics are mediums."

Of all the concepts in this book, this is perhaps the most important for you to understand. Think of a psychic as a local radio station, tuning into the energy of your life. A medium is like an international short-wave radio operator, using their psychic sensitivity to scan for a much more distant signal, one coming from the energetic plane.

Have you ever confused a psychic with a medium? You're definitely not alone. But understanding the difference can help you find exactly what you're looking for.

What is a Psychic Reading?

A psychic reading focuses entirely on you. The psychic links.

The psychic connects with your personal energy field, or aura, to read your story, your past experiences, current emotions, and future potential. The information source is you. This is why psychic readings, often using tools like Tarot cards or psychometry, are oriented toward life guidance.

What is a Mediumship Reading?

A mediumship reading shifts the focus away from you and toward the unseen world. The medium establishes a link with an external, independent consciousness. The information comes through the medium, not from them. The entire process hinges on evidential information, specific, verifiable facts that serve as the spirit's calling card, proving their identity beyond any doubt.

Why This Matters for You (The Sitter)

Knowing this distinction empowers you. If you need life guidance, seek a psychic. If you want to connect with a soul who has passed, a medium is your best means of doing so. Understanding this saves you time, money, and potential heartache, and makes you an informed consumer as you seek a soothing and meaningful experience.

The 'How': Types of Mediumships You'll Encounter

Mental Mediumship: The Inner Senses

In the overwhelming majority of modern readings, communication happens through mental mediumship. This means the medium receives information internally, through their own mind and spiritual senses. These senses, commonly referred to as the "clairs", are the unique ways mediums perceive the presence and messages of the realm of souls. Each medium has different strengths among these abilities, and they often work together in harmony:

- **Clairvoyance (Clear Seeing)**
- **Clairaudience (Clear Hearing)**
- **Clairsentience (Clear Feeling)**
- **Claircognizance (Clear Knowing)**

These spiritual senses are the foundation of how mediums receive and interpret afterlife communication. A more in-depth exploration of each of these "clairs" and how they work can be found in Chapter 3.

Physical Mediumship: An External Phenomenon

It's also important to briefly acknowledge physical mediumship, though it's far less common today. In this form, a spirit manipulates the physical environment to create external effects, such as table-tipping, direct voice phenomena, or the appearance of objects (apports). While dramatic and historically fascinating, this form of mediumship is energy intensive and far more susceptible to fraud. Today, healing-focused, evidential mental mediumship is the cornerstone of legitimate practice.

Managing Your Expectations

The legitimate practice of mediumship today is subtle, evidential, and deeply spiritual. It is not about spectacle or sensationalism, but about quiet moments of truth that bring light into grief. Mediumship is not about telling you what you want to hear. It's about showing you, through deeply personal and specific evidence, that your cherished one still exists, and is still loving you from beyond the veil. The rest of this book will walk you through how this process unfolds and why, for so many, it becomes a restorative truth that changes everything.

So now that you know what mediumship truly is... what might it offer you?

CHAPTER 2

The Spirit World–A Glimpse Beyond the Veil

What happens when we die? It's one of life's most enduring questions, and one that carries deep emotional weight, especially when someone we adore has passed. That our consciousness continues in some form is a belief shared across centuries and continents. But what does that mean, really? And how do we, the living, understand or even attune to those who've passed into that unseen world?

Mediumship offers one way in. But before we dive into how communication happens, it's important to explore where those we have a profound bond go and what kind of world they might now inhabit. This chapter isn't about proving the afterlife, it's about exploring possibilities with open hearts and minds. You don't need to accept every idea as truth. Just let yourself wonder. Let yourself experience.

Have you ever felt something you couldn't explain, but knew, deep down, it meant something?

When I was about 12 years old, my family and I were driving from Germany into Italy. As we were approaching a small town, I suddenly spoke up from the back seat and described in detail what the village ahead looked like. My parents were astonished at the accuracy of my description as we drove through the town. For me, it simply felt natural and normal. More than likely, I was recalling a place I'd been to in another life.

Theories of the Afterlife: A Cross-Cultural Perspective

Every culture has wrestled with the mystery of death. Some envision heaven and hell. Others believe in reincarnation or becoming one with the universe. Some Indigenous traditions speak of the ancestors watching over the living, while Eastern philosophies describe the soul's journey through many lives as a way to evolve.

Despite the differences, these beliefs all point to one shared truth: life doesn't simply end. Something, call it spirit, soul, consciousness, essence, continues. For mediums, this is not a matter of faith but of experience. They regularly speak with personalities who are no longer physically present, who come through with clarity, compassion, and unmistakable presence.

From ancient Egypt to modern Christianity, from Hinduism to Native American traditions, the afterlife has been imagined as a place where we are reunited, healed, or continue our growth. In that way, the realm of souls is less a "place" and more a state of being, vibrational, intelligent, and deeply loving.

What if the afterlife isn't somewhere far away at all, but closer than we ever imagined, just vibrating on a different frequency?

"This connection brought such relief..."

"Sharon, thank you from the bottom of my heart for bringing through this connection and the beautiful messages I so deeply needed to hear. Though things between Jason and me ended on a painful note, and he passed before I ever found closure, this experience lifted a tremendous weight I've carried ever since. Just before our session, I had been speaking to him silently, asking that he be there to greet [our dog] when her time comes—and knowing he heard me has brought such peace." — D.

How Your Loved Ones Continue: The Soul's Journey

When someone we cherish dies, their body ceases to function, but their consciousness doesn't. Think of the body like a vehicle; when it breaks down, the driver steps out and continues on another path. Mediums often describe this transition not as an ending, but as a return, like going home after a long trip.

People in the afterlife don't become omniscient, emotionless beings. They keep their personalities, sense of humor, memories, and especially their enduring devotion to us. They're not watching you 24/7, but they do drop in, especially when you're thinking of them, talking to them, or going through something significant. Sometimes when you suddenly start thinking of them, it may be that they're thinking of you and popping in to say "hello." Their goal isn't to interfere, but to comfort and support you. They have their own growth to tend to, and love acts as a bridge. It keeps the bridge open.

Could it be that love, not death, is the true unbreakable bond between souls?

Not too long after Shah's passing, I had a vivid dream that woke me in tears. In the dream, my parents were driving away from me in a convertible sports car, and Shah was in the back seat with them. I remember screaming at them not to leave me, it felt so final, so devastating. But many months later, I realized the dream wasn't about abandonment. It was about reassurance. It was Spirit's way of showing me that Shah was safe, and that he was with family who loved him. What a blessing that realization turned out to be.

One moment, I was a child in the back seat of my parents' car. Decades later, I was the mother, receiving a dream that rewrote everything I thought I knew.

When Shah was a little boy, he was absolutely crazy about everything that was Batman and The Joker. Especially The Joker. I remember a time when I found a pair of high-top sneakers at J. C.

Penney that had The Joker all over them. Naturally, I purchased them for him!

When these signs arrive, how do you feel in your body? Is it warmth, peace, a sudden knowing? That's your soul recognizing truth.

Shortly after his passing, his sister was in California for a visit. As she was driving, her attention was drawn to look at this particular truck with this name and image!

Another time when I was driving, crying and feeling pretty disconsolate, I asked my son for a sign that he was still around me. Less than a second later, as I was looking ahead, this is what I saw. Yet another example of how spirit can communicate.

Recently I was coming out of the Orlando airport on my way to visit my daughter, an Uber driver pulled up directly in front of me to pick up his fare. This is what I saw. While I know how our loved ones can communicate from the afterlife, I admit I was astonished at seeing this! It was as though Shah was letting me know he was with me during my visit!

There have been many other signs from him over the years. Each one is a joy for me to perceive and receive. They've also been part of my own healing journey too.

Many describe the energetic plane as a place of learning. Imagine schools for the soul, places to reflect, grow, and release earthly pain. Mediums sometimes receive images of gardens, libraries, or communities of light. These are symbolic glimpses, meant to help us understand a realm beyond physical description. What's constant, though, is the feeling: peace, clarity, connectedness.

Who Communicates: Guides, Loved Ones, and the Nature of Spirit

Most of the time, it's loved ones who step forward first in a reading, a parent, sibling, partner, friend, or even a beloved pet. These souls come because the bond you shared with them still lives and breathes in the energetic realm. They often identify themselves with specific, personal details, a silly nickname, a vivid memory, or a heartfelt phrase that only you would recognize. Their purpose is to offer reassurance, comfort, and the reminder that they're still with you.

But Spirit is not limited by our expectations. Sometimes, it's a spirit guide who steps forward, an energy that has been gently nudging you your whole life. These guides may feel angelic, wise, or deeply familiar, even if you don't have a conscious memory of them. Their messages are typically filled with encouragement and insight, helping you grow in your spiritual journey or find clarity in your rebuilding process.

And now and then, people you didn't expect, or perhaps didn't even know well, make their presence known. An ancestor, a distant relative, an acquaintance through shared experiences, or even someone who played a background role in your life. The realm of souls operates with a wider lens than we do, and when these individuals show up, there's always a meaningful reason. Their presence reminds us that heartfelt connection, reconciling, and soul attunements often stretch far beyond what we can perceive.

Have you ever wondered what might happen if you just said "yes" to the possibility of hearing from someone you miss?

Preparing for your Reading

Your role is not to be a passive observer but an active participant. By arriving with an open heart and a genuine desire to establish a link, you contribute your own energy to the process, making it easier for the medium and the spirit to form a strong link. You don't need to be a "believer," but a willingness to listen and an open-minded state of receptivity can make a world of difference. The profound bond you hold with the person you wish to hear from is the very beacon that guides them to the conversation.

If your treasured one has recently passed, I highly recommend waiting at least 3 months before having a reading. Your energy may be very low during that time. The connection is best for both the sitter and medium if they are experienced at a higher energy level during a reading.

In my work as a medium, I've had the privilege of witnessing countless powerful, intimate moments of reconnection. Each reading is unique, but the common thread is always love, pure, restorative, and unwavering.

If you are drawn to explore a reading for yourself, or are curious about how this work might support your own healing, I warmly invite you to visit my website: www.aperfectsoul.com.

There, you'll find more information about what to expect in a reading, how to book, and how to begin connecting with your loved ones in Spirit.

I offer this work from a place of deep reverence, for the Spirit world, for your comfort, and for the bond that never dies.

If you had just five more minutes with someone you love, what would you say? Now imagine they're trying to say it to you.

Why They Communicate: The Enduring Power of Love and Connection

Why do those who have transitioned bother? Why attempt to come through?

The answer is always love.

Spirit communication isn't about curiosity or entertainment. It's about mending and learning to move forward again. Those in the afterlife know the experience of grief. They understand the ache of unfinished conversations and the sharp edges of unresolved relationships. They come to say: I'm still here. I still love you. I'm okay.

Sometimes they come to bring comfort. Sometimes to apologize. Sometimes just to remind you that your life still matters deeply and that they're cheering you on from the other side.

Love is the most powerful energy, transcending time, space, and death. A mediumship reading is simply a moment when that love is given voice again.

Science, Consciousness, and the Survival of the Soul

While personal experiences and spiritual traditions provide deeply moving evidence of life after death, modern science is also beginning to explore what happens when we die, and what might continue.

✦ Consciousness Beyond the Brain

In recent decades, researchers have begun seriously examining whether consciousness might extend beyond physical brain function. Studies conducted by organizations like the University of Virginia's Division of Perceptual Studies (DOPS) have documented compelling cases of children with past life memories, near-death experiences (NDEs), and veridical perception, information people could not have known unless their awareness extended beyond the body.

✦ Near-Death Experiences as Evidence

The International Association for Near-Death Studies (IANDS) has collected thousands of firsthand accounts where individuals clinically pronounced dead later reported vivid, conscious experiences, meeting deceased relatives, reviewing their lives, and returning with transformed perspectives. While no single study proves life after death, the consistency of these reports points toward a non-material continuation of awareness.

✦ Theories in Psychology

The famed psychologist Carl Jung also wrote about death and the survival of consciousness, suggesting that death may not be an end, but a return to a collective, spiritual dimension. He described one of his own near-death experiences as "the most sublime thing" he'd ever known.

Though the scientific world continues to debate these findings, the implications are undeniable: consciousness may not be confined to the brain. If that's true, then the bonds of love may truly transcend the veil of death.

For those grieving, this isn't just science, it's hope.

"She nailed his generous nature..."

"Sharon has a warm, uplifting presence that immediately puts you at ease. She picked up that he loved working with his hands, and

she even mentioned the yellow daffodils he planted in our yard, something so personal it took my breath away. But the most powerful moment came when she heard the word "windward." I knew instantly that he was talking about sailing, and in that moment, I had no doubt it was truly him coming through." —B.

CHAPTER 3

The Mechanics of Communication– How It Works

To the untrained eye, a mediumship reading can seem like magic. How does someone, out of thin air, bring through a detail about your grandmother's handwriting, or mention the inside joke you shared with your brother? The answer isn't magic. It's attunement. Communication with those who have crossed the veil relies on subtle, energetic interaction between three parties: the spirit, the medium, and you, the sitter. And the method is far more nuanced and delicate than most people realize.

I had a vague recollection of a woman visiting my Nana when I was a little girl and that there was a crystal ball involved. My Nana took the woman into the sitting room, closed the door, and that was that. Years later I was talking to my aunt and learned that my Nana had been a psychic medium! Too bad I didn't know that when she was alive. What a conversation or two we would have shared. She is with me now and, thankfully, acts as a guide in my life. ♥

This chapter opens the curtain on what actually happens in a mediumship reading from the medium's perspective, and why your energy and mindset are more important than you may think.

"The evidence was compelling and healing..."

" Sharon brought through a powerful connection with my mother. The evidence she shared was deeply accurate, she captured not only my mother's personality but also the quiet struggles she carried that few ever knew about. The reading was profoundly emotional and brought a level of healing I didn't expect."—V.

The Language of Spirit: Energy and Vibration

Every single thing in the universe, your body, your thoughts, the chair you're sitting on, is made of energy vibrating at different frequencies. When mediums talk about "raising their vibration," they mean elevating their consciousness to match the frequency of the unseen realm, which vibrates at a much higher, subtler rate.

Think of it like tuning a radio dial. The medium is adjusting their inner tuner to find the right station. The spirit is simultaneously "lowering" their frequency so they can be received. When both meet in the middle, when the tuning aligns, that's when the communication begins.

The consciousness beyond doesn't use words the way we do. They communicate through thought, memory, images, emotions, sensations, and symbols. The medium's job is to interpret this energetic stream into something you can understand. It's a translation job, and no translation is ever 100% literal.

The Medium's Toolkit: The Six Clairs and Beyond

Most communication comes through what mediums call "the clairs." Think of these as our ordinary senses being put to use to align with the one in spirit.

- **Clairvoyance (clear seeing):** The medium receives visual images in the mind's eye. It could be a vivid flash of your father's face, or a symbolic red balloon representing a birthday just passed. Once, during a reading, I suddenly saw a man holding a fishing pole, grinning. The client gasped, her grandfather had taught her to fish as a child and always said he'd "cast a line from heaven" one day.
  That image? That was his hello.

- **Clairaudience (clear hearing):** This is the inner sense of hearing, not with the ears, but within the mind. Names, songs, even a whisper like "I'm proud of you" may come through. Once, I heard the jingle of an ice cream truck, which seemed random, until the client told me that her brother, who had passed, used to drive one. It brought her to tears.

- **Clairsentience (clear feeling):** A rush of emotion, a stab of chest pain, a deep belly laugh, these are all ways spirit communicates through feeling. It's like the medium momentarily borrows the spirit's emotions or sensations. During a session, I once felt the unmistakable "fidgetiness" of a man who couldn't sit still. "That's him exactly!" his daughter said.

- **Claircognizance (clear knowing):** This is a sudden, unquestionable knowing, a name, a detail, or even a feeling of "This is what they want you to hear." There's no image or sound, just certainty. It's as if the message drops into the mind fully formed. I've had moments where I simply "knew" the person was a twin, and sure enough, the sitter confirmed it.Mediums might also use other senses, like taste (clairegustance) or smell (clairsalience), especially when spirit wants to bring up a strong memory (like the smell of Dad's cigars or Grandma's favorite soup).

- **Clairalience (clear smelling):** Smelling a familiar cologne or pipe smoke.

- **Clairgustance (clear tasting):** Tasting lemon pie or mint tea, often used to evoke a loved one's favorite treat.

These senses are delicate, like spider silk. They require trust, quiet, and deep listening. Over time, a medium learns which ones are strongest, and how to interpret what they receive with humility and heart.

Symbolism and Interpretation: Spirit's Creative Language

The energetic plane is efficient. Instead of spelling out a message word for word, they often use symbols, memories, and images with emotional charge. A medium might see a red rose, not because the spirit is handing you a rose, but because it represents romantic love, an anniversary, or a name like "Rose."

Interpretation becomes key. Skilled mediums know when to probe deeper, when to trust the first impression, and when to ask for more clarity. It's a dance between what they're receiving and how they share it, without distorting the message.

Being a medium is like being handed puzzle pieces from two people speaking different languages, and trying to build a picture both can understand.

I once had a reading where Spirit showed me a sunflower. I wasn't sure what it meant, so I shared it with the client. She teared up immediately. "My daughter passed last year," she said. "I planted sunflowers in her memory, she loved them." What looked like a simple flower to me was actually her daughter's signature. That moment reminded me: spirit often speaks in symbols, and the heart knows what they mean.

Think of the medium as a translator. The goal isn't perfection, but communication that is experienced as emotionally true and evidentially accurate. Clarity doesn't always come in paragraphs. Sometimes it arrives as a flash. A symbol. A tear. A smile.

How the Sitter's Energy Shapes the Reading

You, the sitter, are not a passive audience member, you're one of the energetic co-creators of the reading. Your emotional openness, willingness to engage, and trust in the process all impact the clarity of the connection.

You're not just receiving the message, you're helping shape it. Like a microphone amplifying a whisper, your openness can make the difference between a muffled noise and a clear voice.

If you come into the reading shut down, combative, or overly skeptical, it creates static. Imagine trying to tune into a distant radio station while driving through a tunnel, it's still there, but will not hear much.

That doesn't mean you have to be a wide-eyed believer. Healthy curiosity is welcomed. But when you're emotionally guarded, grieving deeply, or resistant, it can dim the light that spirit uses to bond.

Mediums are also human. They're not mind-readers; they're heart listeners. Offering feedback, such as "yes," "no," or "I'm not sure", helps spirit refine the message. Silence, while understandable, can sometimes act as a closed door.

"Sharon, the way you brought through my father was extraordinary. Through you, I was able to see the beauty of life as he saw it, and that shifted something deep within me. The message you delivered from him is something I will carry for the rest of my life. It gave me comfort, clarity, and a renewed confidence in my path forward." — M.

Spirit's Role: Bridging Two Worlds

Many people assume that spirit communication is effortless from the other side. It's not. It takes just as much focus and energy for your precious one to communicate as it does for the medium to receive them. *Imagine spirit as sunlight trying to stream through a keyhole. The medium's job is to catch that light and help you recognize its warmth.*

Those in the afterlife may use reference points from the medium's own life to communicate ("show her what my wedding dress looked like"), or they might draw upon shared memories of you and them. The stronger the bond, the clearer the signal. Spirit doesn't forget birthdays! But even distant relatives or quiet personalities can show up with powerful messages.

Just like in life, some who've transitioned are talkative and detailed; others are reserved or symbolic. Some rush forward; others hesitate. But all come with a desire: to reconnect, to help, to heal.

The Flow of a Reading: A Living Conversation

Mediumship readings typically unfold in three parts:

1. **Evidence**–Spirit provides identifying details like personality traits, shared experiences, cause of death, or names.

2. **Message**–A message of unconditional affection, support, reassurance, or closure is shared. Sometimes they speak about your life, but only from a place of care, not command.

3. **Closure**–The energy begins to fade. Spirit may offer one last sign or sentiment, then withdraw gently.

It's important to note that not everything will make sense immediately. Sometimes the evidence becomes clear hours or days later. Those who have transitioned may even reference events that haven't happened yet.

A reading isn't a test, it's a reunion. It's not about performance. It's about presence. And like any heartfelt conversation, it's the emotion and connection that matter most.

What to Remember?

- Mediums don't summon those in the afterlife. Spirit chooses to come.

- You can't control who comes through, but the one who does often has the most important message.

- The process is subtle, profound, and deeply personal. It's a privilege to witness it.

When approached with trust, compassion, and openness, mediumship becomes more than a curiosity. It becomes a reminder that love, and life, are never truly lost.

Here are two examples of readings I did where it shows that the medium does not control what happens in a reading. Both turned out to be soul/higher soul readings. The first was a from a husband who is still in life. This happens sometimes when an individual wants to get a message to their treasured one and doesn't know how to say it in person. The second one was a communication with this lady's higher self.

"Sharon you're incredible! You connected with the energy of someone who means the world to me in this lifetime, what an unexpected and wonderful surprise. Energy truly is everything and everywhere! You shared such specific details about him that were both accurate and delightful to hear, along with a meaningful message from spirit that touched my heart." – A

When a Soul Steps Forward

Occasionally, in a reading, no spirit communicator from the other side comes through right away. Instead, what appears is a presence that feels... familiar. Grounded. Yet elevated.

This is the sitter's own higher self, the soul essence that exists beyond the personality, beyond the wounds or ego. The wise part that knows who you truly are, what you came here to learn, and how far you've already come.

Why would a soul reading happen?

Because sometimes, what is needed most isn't a message from a loved one, but a reconnection with your own deep truth. This kind of session can unfold when you're standing at a crossroads, holding heavy questions, or seeking alignment with your purpose.

A soul reading can bring clarity, comfort, and a kind of spiritual recalibration. It reminds you that you already hold the map within.

These sessions are rare, but beautiful. And they serve as a reminder that whether the message comes from spirit, or from your own soul's wisdom, you are being guided.

"I hope I can fully express the depth and beauty of what today's reading gave me. From the very first word, it was clear this was a soul reading, my own soul speaking through you. I'm so grateful you didn't try to force it into a traditional mediumship session but instead trusted spirit and allowed what truly needed to come forward. What she delivered was a precise, channeled transmission of pure, loving energy.

It's difficult to find the right words to express the gratitude I feel. Your reading moved me to tears. I don't think I've ever felt so deeply seen before. The message you channeled reflected every layer of who I am in this lifetime. I found myself nodding again and again, thinking, Yes... this is me. This is exactly me. It was humbling, powerful, and incredibly encouraging.

This wasn't a surface-level reading about hobbies or personal trivia. This was profound soul-level insight, about how I move through the world as a human being and how I contribute from the essence of my spirit. It reached a deeper dimension, one that touched my inner knowing, far beyond the surface mind.

You ARE a spark. What you brought forward today gave me hope and direction again. I can't thank you enough for this gift. I will carry it forward in my heart, grateful our paths crossed.

No agenda. No ego. Just a clear, pure channel for spirit. Your authenticity speaks for itself. I imagine the guides and angels are overjoyed with how beautifully it all unfolded."-A.

CHAPTER 4

Finding a Reputable Medium

Finding a reputable medium can feel like trying to navigate a crowded room while blindfolded. There are so many voices out there, so many websites and social media pages filled with glowing testimonials and angelic branding. Not all mediums are created equal, and not all who call themselves mediums are truly doing this work with integrity.

When I am giving a reading, it's my job to learn from the spirit what the relationship is with my sitter, if the one who's crossed over chooses to disclose that information. The individual may have other things they discern as more important to say to you during a reading. I ask of the sitter the following questions–*"Would you understand this?"*, *"Can you accept that piece of information?"* or something similar.

This chapter is your guide for navigating the process of choosing someone who is a good fit for you, ethically, energetically, and emotionally. It will help you avoid common pitfalls, recognize red flags, and most importantly, listen to your own inner guidance.

Start with Your Intention

Before you even begin searching for a medium, take a few minutes to get really clear with yourself: Why are you seeking a reading? Are you grieving and hoping to hear from a specific loved one? Are you simply curious? Are you in emotional distress and looking for direction or soothing?

Mediumship is not therapy, yet it can be therapeutic. It's essential to know what your hopes are before you invite someone into your consecrated space. Setting your intention helps guide your energy and helps spirit align with that energy too.

Try journaling your intention in one or two sentences. Do you want to hear from your grandmother, the one who always said she'd find a way to reach you after she passed? Or are you hoping to find peace after a difficult goodbye?

Imagine walking into a reading, not with a checklist, but with a softly held hope: *"Please let me know you're okay."* That gentle clarity can make all the difference in what unfolds.

Not only will this help you focus your search, but it will also be helpful if you speak to a prospective medium in advance.

Where to Look: Referrals, Organizations, and Online Presence

Once your intention is clear, start exploring.

1. **Referrals from trusted sources:** If you know someone who's had a powerful and restorative experience with a medium, ask who they went to. One I knew resulted from my frequenting a local spiritual center. Personal referrals are gold.

2. **Reputable directories and organizations:** Look into mediums listed with organizations like the Spiritualist National Union (SNU), the National Association of Spiritualist Churches (NASC), or other ethics-based spiritual institutions. While membership doesn't guarantee excellence, it often indicates a level of training and accountability.

3. **Professional websites and social media:** A genuine medium should have an online presence that resonates with clarity, integrity, and accessibility. Look for testimonials, information about their training, approach and values.

4. **Podcasts, interviews, or YouTube appearances:** How do they speak about spirit? Do they come across as grounded, compassionate, and human? These unscripted moments can reveal a lot.

For example, imagine you hear a medium in a podcast interview, and their voice feels steady, kind, grounded. Maybe they don't "wow" you with drama, but something about their presence feels safe. That sense of calm can often tell you more than any testimonial.

Remember: you are not looking for flash or glamour. You are looking for warmth, professionalism, humility, and evidence of real skill.

You might wonder, "Is it okay to ask these things?" The answer is yes. A true professional will welcome your questions. Imagine calling a prospective medium and they respond warmly, "Of course- ask me anything you need." That openness is often your first confirmation that you're in the right hands.

"From beginning to end, I felt an affirmation of love..."

"You left out all interpretation and shared the feelings you were receiving as evidence... After my loved one left, you reached out and, in short, gave me an energetic hug that allowed me to remain in the present with breath." — A.

A Smart Sitter's Guide to Finding a Reputable Medium

Asking a few simple questions can help you understand how a medium works and whether they're a good fit for you. Here are some examples:

How long have you been practicing mediumship?

What kind of training have you received (and from whom)?

Do you specialize in evidential mediumship?

What is your code of ethics?

What should I expect during a session?

Do you record the session?

Can I read testimonials or reviews?

What is your cancellation/rescheduling policy?

Red Flags

Guarantees of specific outcomes or contacts

Vague or overly general information

High-pressure sales tactics or upselling

Claiming to remove curses or spells

Predicting death, illness, or financial ruin

Discouraging second opinions or other healing modalities

Your instinct is your best guide. If something seems off, honor that. Mediumship should always feel like a safe, grounded, and respectful experience.

Have there been moments in your life where you knew something without being told? Could that same knowing guide you now?

Trusting Your Intuition in the Selection Process

Choosing a medium isn't just about credentials, it's about resonance. You may experience a sense of ease, trust, or curiosity when you look at their photo, read their website, or hear them speak.

Your intuition knows. Even if you're grieving or nervous, take a moment to sit with the emotion: Does this person feel kind? Clear? Safe? If your answer is "I'm not sure," pause. Ask yourself: Do I feel calmer or more anxious after engaging with them online? Does their energy feel inviting or performative?

You might recall how, in another area of life, your gut led you toward a trustworthy friend, or away from someone who didn't feel right. Trust the same wisdom here.

Don't underestimate the importance of timing either. If a reading is delayed or rescheduled, trust that spirit might be orchestrating things for your highest good. Mediumship often works in synchronistic ways.

What to Expect from a Professional Reading

Once you've selected your medium, here's what a professional experience typically looks like:

Clear boundaries: The medium will explain how the reading works, how long it will last, and what they can or cannot answer.

An emphasis on evidence: They will begin by bringing forward details from the spirit communicator, names, personality traits, memories, shared experiences, etc.

Gentle delivery: Even if emotional or difficult topics arise, the tone will remain respectful and compassionate.

Ethical closure: The reading will end with clarity and care. You'll be encouraged to take time afterward to reflect or journal.

You should leave feeling more peaceful, more centered, not confused, drained, or emotionally manipulated.

What does feeling "peaceful" mean to you? If you left a session and felt lighter, what would that look like in your day-to-day life?

You Have the Right To...

Let's be clear, you are never at the mercy of a reading. As a sitter, you have rights, and a professional medium will honor them. You have the right to:

Ask questions before booking.

Cancel or reschedule.

Decline a message that feels inappropriate or off.

Ask for clarity or repetition.

Choose to record the reading to keep it confidential. (note-I record all sessions-a) for legal purposes. b) In the event the client loses their copy, I can provide them with another one.)

Walk away if you feel unsafe or uncomfortable.

Mediumship is a hallowed experience. It should be a doorway to help uplift you, not a detour into confusion or dependency.

Closing Thoughts: Choose with Care, Receive with Trust

There is no rush. Finding a reputable medium is like finding a good therapist, mentor, or spiritual companion, it's worth taking your time. The right medium will make you feel seen, respected, and empowered. They won't tell you what to do or try to be your spiritual guru. They'll simply open the door, so you and your precious ones in the afterlife can meet in that quiet, reverent place of communing with each other.

Remember, you don't have to subscribe to a particular belief system to benefit from this work. Mediumship doesn't replace your spirituality, it can simply deepen your relationship with love, memory, and meaning.

Whether you consider it faith, energy, or mystery, the goal is the same: healing.

And when you find the right one? The experience will stay with you forever.

Additional Considerations When Choosing a Medium

Understanding Different Mediumship Styles

Not all mediums work the same way, and understanding different styles can help you align your expectations with the right practitioner. Some mediums are quiet and reflective; others are animated and conversational. Some stay very evidence-focused, sticking to validations before offering a message. Others blend intuitive insight with spirit communication. There's no one "right" way, only what works for you.

You might resonate more with someone who takes a spiritual, almost ministerial tone, or with someone more grounded and humorous. Mediums are human, after all, and their personalities shine through. Just as in everyday life, your rapport with someone makes a difference.

Some questions you might consider:

Do I want someone who will hold a calm, peaceful space, or someone who brings a lighter, more energetic tone?

Am I looking for evidential accuracy only, or do I want spiritual guidance as well?

Would I prefer a private one-on-one reading or a group demonstration?

The more specific you are about your desires, the more likely it is you'll find someone who complements your energy and intentions.

Traits of an Ethical Medium

Respectful of emotional vulnerability

Transparent about limitations

Willing to explain the process

Focused on healing, not fear

Willing to say, "I'm not getting anything right now"

Empowers the sitter rather than fostering dependency

A Note on "Celebrity" Mediums

While some well-known mediums have earned their reputations through years of practice and public visibility, don't assume that fame equals quality. Many talented mediums operate quietly and ethically outside of the spotlight.

Some clients seek big names, expecting the best possible experience. And while it's exciting to meet with a "celebrity" medium, remember: their calendars are often booked months in advance, and the price tag may reflect their notoriety, not necessarily a stronger link to those who have transitioned.

Don't overlook the gems in your local community or those working online who may have less visibility but more availability and a deep commitment to their work.

Virtual vs. In-Person Readings

In our digitally oriented world, many mediumship readings are now offered online, through Zoom, Skype, or even over the phone. You might wonder: Does it still work if we're not in the same room?

The answer is a resounding yes. Because spirit communication is energetic, not physical, mediums don't need to be in your physical presence. What matters is intention and connection. Many people report just as powerful, emotional, and validating experiences online as they do in person.

That said, your personal comfort matters. Some people are more at ease in their own homes during a virtual reading. Others crave the energetic presence of an in-person setting. There's no right or wrong, only what supports your sense of trust and safety.

For example, I only do Zoom readings. Those in the afterlife are everywhere. They don't need a specific location to get their messages through! This works especially well for people who don't live nearby or who live in another country or state.

Post-Reading Practices: Integrating the Experience

Choosing the right medium is only the first step. What you do after the reading matters just as much.

Give yourself time to process. A reading can bring up deep emotions. Set aside quiet time afterward to reflect, journal, or simply rest.

Avoid immediate analysis. Don't rush to dissect every detail right away. Let things settle. Sometimes the evidence becomes clear hours or even days later.

Return to the recording. If the reading was recorded (with your consent), listen again a few days later. You might hear things you missed the first time.

Notice synchronicities. Often, the unseen realm will continue communicating through signs, dreams, or meaningful coincidences in the days following the reading. Stay open.

Mediumship is a conversation with the invisible. It echoes long after the reading ends.

What helps you integrate emotional experiences, quiet reflection, music, writing, prayer? How might you bring those into the hours after a reading?

In Case of Disappointment: What to Do When It Doesn't Land

Even with the most reputable medium, sometimes a reading doesn't resonate. This does not reflect the medium's ability or the fact that the spirit did not show up. There are many reasons a reading may feel "off."

The person you hoped to connect with may not have come through.

You may have been emotionally closed off without realizing it.

The medium might have had a tough day energetically.

The timing may not have been right, spirits have their own timing and wisdom.

If this happens:

Take a breath. Don't judge the entire experience at the moment.

Reflect later. Did anything shift in the hours or days afterward?

Consider giving it another try, with a different medium, or at another time.

A disappointing reading doesn't mean mediumship doesn't work. It simply means that, like any human experience, it's imperfect. But often, even in a "miss," those in the energetic realm may be working behind the scenes in ways you don't yet understand.

I once had a client who left a session feeling unsure, nothing had landed clearly in the moment. But two days later, she emailed to say that a name I'd mentioned repeatedly was actually her father's birth name, which she'd forgotten was on his passport. The "miss" turned into a moment of astonished recognition long after the reading had ended.

Want to experience this firsthand? I invite you to explore the resources and readings I offer on my website, www.aperfectsoul.com, where you can learn more about evidential mediumship and schedule a session if your heart feels called.

Final Thoughts

Finding a reputable medium is a process of both discernment and trust. Use your intellect and your intuition. Seek evidence and listen to your gut. Choose someone whose presence feels respectful, grounded, and humble, someone who makes room for your emotions and treats your experience as reverent.

Mediumship at its best reminds us that our eternal bond transcends death, and that healing is always available to us. When you find the right medium, you'll know, not just because of what they say, but because of how you feel.

CHAPTER 5

Opening the Door Within

Developing Your Own Intuition and Connection to Spirit

You don't have to be a professional medium to receive guidance from the spirit world. In truth, you were born with the ability to sense, feel, and even communicate with energy beyond what your physical eyes can see. The door has always been there, it just needs to be gently opened.

This chapter isn't about turning you into a medium overnight. Instead, it's about helping you remember what your soul already knows: you are naturally intuitive, and you are already connected. The spirit world is not reserved for a chosen few. It is here for all of us, quietly, patiently, lovingly waiting for us to notice.

Let's walk through how to open that inner door together.

Trust Begins in Stillness

Most of us move through life in a constant hum of activity, thought, and distraction. We're checking our phones, managing responsibilities, running errands. But intuitive awareness doesn't shout, it whispers. And if you're constantly surrounded by noise, both external and internal, those whispers will be drowned out.

The very first step in strengthening your intuitive connection is creating space to listen.

Try this:

Start with five minutes a day. Turn off the television. Put your phone aside. Sit somewhere quiet. Breathe. Let your awareness drop from your head into your heart. You don't have to "do" anything. Just be. Let the silence become your teacher. This is where spirit can find you, when you become present.

Many people expect intuition to feel grand or dramatic, but most times, it's soft and subtle. A gentle nudge. A thought that doesn't feel like your own. A knowing that arises for no logical reason. These are your soul's language cues. Your job is to notice them.

I remember one quiet morning when I was feeling uncertain about a big decision. I wasn't thinking about Spirit at all, just sipping my morning coffee in silence. Then, clear as day, a thought popped into my head: "Not yet." It wasn't dramatic or loud. It felt calm and firm. I sat with it, wrote it down, and let it be. Two weeks later, new information came to light that confirmed that the delay was the right path. That moment taught me that our deepest wisdom often comes in the gentlest forms, when we're quiet enough to hear it.

Strengthen the Muscle of Inner Sensing

Your intuition is like a muscle, it gets stronger with regular use. And just like physical muscles, we all have different strengths. Some people "see" images when they close their eyes. Others "hear" inner words or phrases. You might "feel" certain emotions or bodily sensations. Or maybe you just "know" things and can't explain why.

You might be folding laundry and suddenly see an image of your grandmother's hands or her favorite necklace (clairvoyance). Or while driving, you "hear" the words "slow down" in a voice that isn't quite yours (clairaudience). Perhaps you walk into a room and feel a wave of anxiety or warmth that isn't your own (clairsentience). Or you might simply "know" that your cousin is struggling, even if you haven't spoken in months (claircognizance). These moments may feel fleeting, but they're glimpses of your intuitive language.

Each of these is valid. Each is real. You don't have to be like anyone else.

Try this:

Set an intention before bed each night: "I am open to guidance." Keep a notebook nearby. As soon as you wake up, even if it's the middle of the night, write anything you remember from your dreams, thoughts that pop in, or sensations that linger. These early impressions often carry insights from your higher self or spirit loved ones.

Another simple practice is to close your eyes during the day and ask a question like: "What do I need to know right now?" Then stay still. Pay attention to what arises, not just in your mind, but in your body, your feelings, your surroundings. Your answer might come as a picture, a phrase, a memory, or even a song lyric that pops into your head. With practice, you'll begin to recognize the signature of your own intuitive language.

Create Sacred Rituals for Connection

If you come from a specific religious or cultural background, consider how your own traditions already honor communication with the unseen. Lighting a yahrzeit candle, offering a silent prayer, walking a labyrinth, visiting a gravesite, or playing a favorite hymn, these can all serve as sacred bridges.

This work doesn't have to conflict with your beliefs. Mediumship is just one doorway among many. If it feels respectful and healing to you, then it belongs.

Ritual is how we make the invisible feel tangible. You don't need incense, crystals, or candles (though you can use them if you enjoy them). What you do need is sincerity. Spirit doesn't respond to perfection, it responds to your heartfelt intention.

Creating a daily or weekly ritual invites spirit closer, and more importantly, it signals to your own inner being that this connection matters to you. Rituals don't have to happen at an altar or in a dimly lit room. You might take a slow, mindful walk outdoors and ask Spirit to speak through nature, a birdcall, a breeze, a feather on the path. Others find a deep connection through creative expression: painting, playing music, dancing, or even gardening can become sacred acts when done with intention. One woman I worked with plays a specific piano piece every Sunday morning, "for her dad," she says, and always feels his presence in the room. Spirits don't need ceremony, they just need sincerity.

Try this:

Choose a quiet time each day or week to sit, reflect, and reach out. You might place a photo of a loved one on a small table, light a candle, and simply say aloud, "I welcome your presence." Then sit in stillness for a few moments. Ask for a sign, a dream, or a message, and then go about your day with trust that it will arrive when the time is right.

You can also write letters to spirit. This is a beautiful and healing practice. Pour out your heart onto the page. Ask your questions. Express your gratitude. And then listen. Often, the answer will come through your own writing, almost as if your pen is being gently guided.

Notice the Nudges (and Don't Brush Them Off)

One of the most common ways people block their intuitive growth is by dismissing their inner nudges. You get a feeling to call a friend, and you ignore it. You think of your grandmother out of the blue, and shrug it off as coincidence. You dream of a past event, and forget it by breakfast.

One afternoon, I kept thinking of a woman I hadn't spoken to in months. I brushed it off, telling myself I'd call later. The feeling wouldn't leave me. Finally, I picked up the phone, and she burst into tears. "I was just sitting here praying for someone to talk to," she said. That call changed both of our days. It reminded me: intuition is often Spirit's way of loving someone through you.

The more you dismiss, the quieter those messages become.

The more you honor those brief moments, the louder and clearer they get. Those on the other side absolutely love when we acknowledge the signs they give us.

Try this:

Begin keeping an "intuition log." Anytime something unusual or out-of-the-blue happens, whether it's a synchronicity, a feeling you followed, a dream, or even just a thought that proved accurate, write it down. Over time, you'll see a pattern forming. A client of mine named Karen began journaling every morning for just ten minutes. At first, it was a blur of random thoughts. But within a few weeks, she noticed a recurring theme: butterflies. In dreams, on walks, even doodled in the margins of her pages. Her mother had loved butterflies. That insight opened the door to deeper communication, and soon, Karen began receiving specific messages and feelings she attributed to her mom.

Another client, David, kept a nightly log of anything unusual he sensed, whether it was a hunch, a feeling, or a moment of synchronicity. Here's an excerpt from one of his early entries:

Journal Entry–March 14

"Woke up at 3:03 a.m. with the name 'Eleanor' in my mind. Don't know any Eleanors... but it felt important."

Two weeks later, his cousin mentioned their grandmother's real name had been Eleanor, though they had always called her Nellie. That moment shifted everything for David, he began to trust that Spirit was, indeed, reaching through.

You'll start to trust that these nudges are not random. They are your inner guidance system. Spirit's calling card. Proof that you are already connected.

Release the Pressure to "Be Right"

One of the biggest blocks to intuitive development is fear of getting it wrong. We doubt ourselves. We want to be accurate. We worry about looking foolish. All of that pressure chokes the natural flow of intuition and spiritual connection.

Intuition doesn't thrive in a test, it blooms in trust.

Give yourself permission to be a beginner. To be human. To make mistakes. That's how you learn. Spirit isn't grading you. In fact, they're gently celebrating your every step forward.

Try this:

If you feel guided to do something loving or kind, act on it. If a name pops into your head, reach out to that person. If you feel drawn to take a new route home, try it. The point isn't to be right. The point is to be responsive. When you act on small intuitive nudges without pressure or fear, you become more aligned with the rhythm of your soul, and with the whispers of spirit.

Intuition isn't something you call up-it's more of something you simply surrender to. It's not forced; rather, you feel it. When you start paying attention to it the magic begins to happen for you.

You Are Already Wired for Connection

You don't need to "become" intuitive. You already are.

You don't need a special title to feel close to your loved ones in spirit.

You don't need to perform miracles to feel the sacredness of your own soul.

What you need is Stillness. Curiosity. Practice. And most of all, Trust.

Whether your goal is to develop your connection for personal comfort or to explore mediumship more deeply, you are on holy ground. The doorway is within you. And every time you open your heart, sit in quiet, or say a simple "hello," the spirit world is listening, and responding.

So, keep going. Keep opening. Keep listening. You are doing beautifully.

CHAPTER   6

Grief as a Sacred Invitation

Transformation Through Loss

No one is ever quite prepared for the avalanche of emotion that follows a loss. Grief is not a polite visitor, it crashes through the heart like a storm, rearranging everything in its path. And yet, beneath its devastation lies a quiet invitation: to deepen, to awaken, to grow.

Viewed through the lens of spirit, grief is not a punishment or a life sentence, it is a profound passage. It reshapes us. It burns away what is unnecessary and carves space within us for greater love, deeper wisdom, and unexpected purpose.

When someone we love leaves this world, we are left with a choice: to remain closed in pain or to allow that pain to become the birthplace of transformation. In this chapter, I invite you to see grief as more than sorrow, it is a sacred teacher.

Moving Beyond Mourning: Honoring with Intention

Traditional memorials have their place, flowers, photos, headstones. But your relationship with someone you love doesn't end when their physical presence does. It changes form, yes, but it continues.

There are infinite, meaningful ways to honor your loved one beyond the expected. You can celebrate them through living rituals, personal acts of remembrance that are as unique as they were.

Here are a few ideas:

Create a sacred corner in your home. Place a candle, a favorite object of theirs, a handwritten letter, or even something playful that reminds you of their personality. This is not about grief on display, it's about connection. It becomes a place you can go to sit, reflect, and feel close.

Celebrate anniversaries in a new way. Instead of marking the day with silence or sorrow, do something that reflects their joy. Cook their favorite meal, play their favorite music, donate to a cause they cared about, or take a walk in nature and speak their name aloud.

Start a tradition. One woman I know writes a letter to her son on his birthday every year, then tucks it into a special journal.

Another releases butterflies each spring in memory of her sister. The point is not the activity, it's the intentional love behind it.

Imagine a man who hikes the same forest trail every spring, scattering wildflower seeds in memory of his late wife, she used to say that wildflowers were "nature's happy accidents." That's his way of keeping her joy alive.

Do you want to create a tradition of your own? Or simply whisper their name into the wind? There's no wrong way to remember.

When you turn grief into a gesture of devotion, you bring spirit closer. These rituals are not about clinging, they are about continuing. They tell your loved one, "You still matter here. You are remembered, cherished, and part of my life."

Holding Your Knowing with Confidence

In a world that prizes logic over mystery, your belief in spirit may feel vulnerable at times, especially when others don't understand.

You may face skepticism from strangers or, harder still, from those closest to you. I've experienced this myself.

For those grounded in religious or traditional frameworks, remember: honoring spirit doesn't have to contradict your beliefs.

Many faiths speak of resurrection, angels, visions, and dreams as channels of divine presence. Mediumship is simply one expression of that eternal connection.

If you pray, keep praying. If you sing, keep singing. Let this be an extension of your devotion, not a replacement for it.

Someone very close to me once told me that my connection to spirit goes against their newly embraced religious beliefs. And yet, to me, this is where irony lives. The very book they lean on, the Bible, tells the story of a man who died and returned, speaking not only to his mother but to travelers, friends, and followers. A man who brought another dead man back to life. A man who conversed openly with an unseen God and encouraged others to do the same. Then 40 days later he rises in the air to who really knows where.

If one can accept those accounts as truth, why is it so difficult to believe that all souls, not just a chosen few, continue to exist and communicate beyond this life?

The truth is this: belief is not about proving anything to anyone else. It's about trusting what resonates deeply within you. It's about honoring the messages, signs, dreams, and feelings that are too consistent, too personal, too healing to be dismissed.

So, when doubts arise, yours or others', breathe into your own clarity. You don't need to argue or convert. Just be still and grounded in what you know to be true. The heart recognizes truth long before the mind catches up.

Reflect for a moment: Have you ever had an experience, an unexplainable sign, a feeling, a dream, that felt real beyond logic?

You don't need to prove it to anyone. Truth doesn't demand validation. It simply wants to be honored.

The Healing Power of Forgiveness in Spirit

One of the most life-altering experiences that can occur through spiritual connection is the ability to find peace with someone who hurt you.

In life, those wounds often remain unresolved. But in spirit, healing is not only possible, it is offered with deep sincerity.

I know this intimately.

My own mother was a deeply wounded woman. An alcoholic. Explosive. Extremely violent. As a child, I bore the weight of her pain, absorbed it, reacted to it, and carried it far beyond her lifetime. But something extraordinary happened when I began my journey into mediumship.

She came through.

Not with excuses, but with awareness. With understanding. With tears.

She showed me images from her own childhood, of instability, of trauma, of unacknowledged mental illness. She expressed regret for how her unhealed suffering had shaped her actions. And then, with more emotion than I ever witnessed from her in life, she told me how proud she is of who I've become. She marveled at the way I've broken generational cycles. She recognized the difference between us, and celebrated it.

Have you ever wished someone would say, "I'm sorry" long after it was too late to hear it from their lips? What if that apology could still find you, from the other side?

Healing doesn't always arrive on time. But it can still arrive.

That moment shifted everything. Not because it changed the past, but because it gave it context. It gave it meaning. It gave me peace.

When someone in spirit acknowledges their impact and offers a genuine apology, it releases a pressure that may have lived inside you for decades. It doesn't excuse the behavior, but it softens your grip on it. It allows love to rise in the space where pain once stood.

Forgiving someone in spirit is not about forgetting. It's about freeing yourself. It's about letting their evolution support your own.

Discovering Purpose Through Loss

Sometimes, the most life-altering changes arrive on the back of unimaginable pain. For me, as mentioned before, that was the loss of my son.

No mother expects to bury her child. When he passed, my world broke open. The grief was unimaginable, but so was the love that remained. I couldn't let go of him. I didn't want to. And that longing, that desire to stay close, led me to something unexpected: the discovery that our bond had not ended. It had simply changed form.

Now, I live a life I never imagined, bringing messages of comfort and validation to others, helping people rediscover hope and peace. My son's legacy is not only one of memory, it's one of purpose.

You may be reading this wondering what your purpose is, or how to find meaning after a loss. The truth is that grief strips us down to our essence. It reveals what matters. It invites us to ask questions we never asked before.

And sometimes, the answers come not from the mind, but from the soul.

What if your pain is pointing to something deeper, something your soul is ready to claim?

You may not need to start a business, write a book, or change the world. But perhaps you're here to love differently now. To see others more clearly. To become the person you wished had walked into your life during your own hardest moment.

I once worked with a woman whose sister had died unexpectedly. At first, her grief was all-consuming. But over time, she began painting again, something she hadn't done since childhood. She told me, "Every time I paint, I feel like my sister is looking through my eyes, reminding me what joy feels like."

That wasn't a performance of healing. That was her sacred return to life. That was purpose, rediscovered through pain.

Ask yourself: What has your loss taught you? What has it revealed in you? What are you now called to do, say, offer, or create that you wouldn't have otherwise?

It doesn't have to be public. It doesn't have to be grand. Maybe it's simply loving more intentionally. Listening more deeply. Supporting someone else who is grieving. Writing. Planting. Speaking the truth.

Let your loss sculpt your purpose, not as a scar, but as a sacred mark of becoming.

What is one thing your grief has taught you about who you truly are?

What would your loved one say if they could see how far you've come?

What do you now know in your bones that you didn't know before loss cracked you open?

Grief as Teacher, Spirit as Companion

As painful as loss is, it awakens us. It strips away illusion. It calls us to live more fully, more honestly, more tenderly. It reminds us that life is fragile, but love is unbreakable.

When we meet grief not just with resistance, but with reverence, it becomes something holy. It brings us to our knees, not in despair, but in humility. It breaks our hearts open wide enough for light to enter.

And from that space, something remarkable happens: we change. We deepen. We remember what matters. We find strength we didn't know we had.

Are you willing to let grief shape you gently, rather than break you completely?

Can you imagine that the love you still feel is not a memory, but a message?

And we hear the whisper: *"I'm still here."*

CHAPTER 7

Soul Contracts, Life Purpose & Why Some Deaths Feel "Too Soon"

There are happenings in life that split us in two, the life we had before, and the life we are forced to live after. Moments that detonate on an otherwise ordinary day and scatter the pieces of our world across a landscape we no longer recognize. A ringing phone at 2:17 a.m. A police officer at the door, hat in hand. A doctor who takes a careful breath before speaking. In those moments, time doesn't just stop, it collapses. And every story we thought we were living changes forever.

When someone we love dies, especially suddenly, tragically, or long before what we would call "their time", the human heart demands answers. *Why did this happen? Why them? Why now? What possible purpose could this pain serve?*

There are no easy answers. There are though deeper truths.

Across many readings, I have heard from souls in Spirit who explain, why some lives feel unbearably short, why suffering exists at all, and why even the most painful goodbyes are not random or meaningless. Again and again, Spirit has shown me something extraordinary:

Life is not an accident.

We are not dropped onto this earth as a roll of cosmic dice. Before we are born, we make soul choices. We participate in the architecture of our own lives. We come into this lifetime carrying intentions, purpose, and agreements. These are often called **soul contracts.**

Although some may recoil at the idea, as if anyone would choose pain, what I've learned is this: **the soul chooses growth, and growth often requires contrast.**

The soul does not fear love, loss, or even death. It understands what our human selves forget, **that death is not the end of us. For peace of mind it's important to remember this point.**

What Exactly Is a Soul Contract?

A soul contract is not a punishment document or karmic debt ledger. It is not fate in the sense of rigid predetermination. A soul contract is far more loving, intelligent, and dynamic. Think of it as a

blueprint of spiritual potential, a plan we design with other souls before we incarnate to create meaningful growth and impact.

Before we are born, our soul chooses:

- The **themes** we will experience, healing, courage, truth, love, grief, expansion.
- The **lessons** we want to master, self-worth, forgiveness, resilience, compassion.
- The **souls** we agree to travel with, some as friends, lovers, teachers, or even challengers.
- The **experiences** that will awaken us to who we really are.

Some souls volunteer to love us then leave us, to act as catalysts (as in my case). Some agree to stay by our side through life, to act as anchors. Some agree to break us open, not to destroy us, but to **transform** us.

And yes, **some souls choose short lives.** Not because they are being punished or because they have failed in some cosmic way, because **their purpose is measured not in time, but in impact.** This is a hard fact to accept initially.

The Short Life With a Big Purpose–Ethan's Story

I once read for a mother named Claire who came into my office looking like she hadn't taken a full breath in weeks. Her five-year-old son, Ethan, had passed away due to complications from a congenital heart defect. Her first words to me were sharp and pained:

"Don't tell me this happened for a reason. There is no reason good enough for this."

I didn't try to change her mind. I proceed with respect, never correction.

When Ethan came through, he didn't speak in grand spiritual jargon. He didn't try to soothe. Instead, he showed me a scene: **a circle of light**, souls preparing to incarnate. I saw Ethan selecting his mother, full of eagerness and devotion. He knew his life would be short. He knew she would suffer. But he also knew she would awaken, and in **her awakening, she would awaken others.**

Through Claire's pain, she eventually began speaking at children's hospitals, advocating for better care for medically fragile children. That turned into a foundation. That foundation has now helped thousands of families. Families who otherwise would have been crushed by medical debt and despair.

In our session, Ethan said to her:

"You didn't fail me. I fulfilled my purpose. I came to build something bigger than a body could hold."

He didn't come here to live a long life.

He came here to ignite one.

But What About Free Will? Do We Really Choose Everything?

No. We don't choose everything. Some events are part of a soul agreement; others unfold through the free will of ourselves and others. Life is not scripted line by line, it is **co-created.**

Think of life like a journey from the East Coast to the West Coast. Your soul contract sets the destination. It will also present major intersections, moments of change, challenge, and growth. But your free will determines how you travel:

- Do you resist or evolve?
- Do you love or shut down?
- Do you repeat old patterns or choose something new?
- Do you numb, deny, and avoid, or heal, awaken, and rise?

The path can be gentle, or brutal. It can be conscious, or unconscious. But **the invitations continue until the lesson is embodied.**

When Death Feels Like a Violation of the Plan–Suicide, Overdose, Tragedy

There are few things heavier than losing someone to suicide or overdose. The grief is tangled with guilt, torment, questions that won't quit. *Could I have stopped it? Why didn't I see the signs? Are they okay? Are they in peace? She/he could have saved him/her.*

I want to be clear: there is **no punishment in the afterlife. There is only truth and healing.** Souls who cross in this way are not banished to darkness or held in cosmic judgment. They are met, gently, with restoration and compassion.

I once read for a woman whose brother, Michael, took his life after a lifelong battle with depression. She sat rigid, afraid to breathe, afraid to hope. Before she spoke, Michael came through. He showed me a mountain with a massive boulder strapped to his back. He said:

"I didn't want to leave. I just couldn't figure out a peaceful way to stay."

He didn't leave because he didn't love his family. He left because he was exhausted. **Pain clouded his ability to see a future.**

Was that ending in his soul contract? In part. The option was there. But like many elements of our soul agreements, **they are conditional, not forced.** Michael's passing was not a failure, it became a turning point. His sister began a suicide awareness program that quite literally saved lives.

Pain, transmuted, becomes purpose.

Spirit has shown me something again and again:

Not every soul comes here for longevity. Some come for precision.

Some come to be healers of hearts through their absence.

Some come to inspire through memory.

Some come to teach the urgency of love.

Some come to guide us *from the other side*, not by leaving us, but by leading us forward. *(This was the case for me after my son passed away.)*

The Death That Changes Everyone–Daniel's Story

Olivia lost her fiancé, Daniel, in a motorcycle accident six weeks before their wedding. He was young, strong, full of life. When I first sat with her, her eyes looked like shattered glass, beautiful, but broken from an impact too sudden to process.

Daniel came through with clarity. His first message to her was:

"Our love is not done. You are not done. I still choose you, differently now."

He showed her that his soul contract was not to grow old, but to serve as a **catalyst**. Through losing him, Olivia began a journey she never expected, she now helps others heal through grief, speaking around the country and teaching parents, partners, and widows that connection continues beyond death.

Some lives don't unfold the way we imagined, yet it is **exactly** as the soul planned.

The Sacred Role of Soul Groups

We do not travel through lifetimes alone. We incarnate in **soul groups**, a collection of souls who repeatedly share lifetimes together in different roles. Your daughter may have been your mother before. Your son may have been your teacher. Your best friend may have been your husband in another life.

Within soul groups, there are often:

- **Primary soulmates**–constant companions across lifetimes.
- **Karmic catalysts**–those who force us to grow, ready or not.
- **Destiny partners**–those who arrive right on time to open a door.
- **Soul teachers**–those who hurt us, not to punish us, but to wake us.

Sometimes one member of a soul group agrees, before birth, to be the one who will **leave early** in order to awaken the others still on earth. *(I highly recommend reading The Little Soul and The Sun: A Children's Parable by Neale Donald Walsch)*

This is neither abandonment nor betrayal. This is a **sacred act of service** from one soul to another.

Love Never Ends-A Personal Truth

I know the truths in this chapter not just as a medium, but as a mother, as a woman, as a soul who has walked through grief and emerged with the unshakeable knowing that love is eternal. That our relationships do not end, they change form. And our loved ones do not disappear when they leave this world, they move beside us, just beyond the veil, still loving us, still helping us, still guiding us. It's as simple as stepping out of this lifetime into the next one into a higher, purer energy where love prevails.

Why Some Deaths Feel "Too Soon"

What is "too soon" from the human perspective often aligns perfectly with the soul's timing. **The soul does not measure a life in years, but in purpose.** Some lives are long because they need time to unfold. Others are brief because they come to deliver a single, powerful message:

Love now.

Do not wait.

Heal now.

Forgive now.

Live awake.

No life is wasted. No death is meaningless. Some souls complete their purpose in 90 years. Others complete it in 9 months. And though both departures create different ripples of grief, **each life is whole. Each life is sacred. Each life matters.**

The Threads We Cannot See

I once read for a man named Thomas whose father died when he was a child. Growing up fatherless hardened him, and he carried decades of resentment and abandonment pain. In his reading, his father came forward and shared that he did not pass *from* Thomas, he passed *for* Thomas.

Before his passing, his father had been trapped in alcoholism, unable to heal, unable to love fully. His message stunned Thomas:

"If I had stayed, I would have hurt you. My leaving broke you for a while, but it saved you for life."

Broken is not the opposite of whole. Broken is the beginning of open. And many souls agree, before birth, to play roles that awaken love, strength, and truth in the ones they leave behind.

We don't always see those threads until much later, but they are there.

Healing Across Lifetimes

Some deaths reopen ancient grief. When someone leaves this life and you feel shattered beyond what seems reasonable, it may be because **your souls have shared lifetimes of connection**. Losing them reopens a wound your soul has carried long before this body was born.

But here is the hope: **healing also echoes across lifetimes.** Every tear shed with awareness, every act of forgiveness, every moment of love chosen over fear, **heals not just you, but every version of you that has ever lived.** Every ancestor still carrying pain. Every descendant yet to be born.

Love is not limited by time. Neither is healing.

How to Heal Through the Lens of Soul Contracts

Understanding soul contracts intellectually is one thing. Living with your heart shattered open is another. So how do you **heal** with this awareness? How do you endure loss when every part of your body aches? How do you find meaning without diminishing your pain?

You really don't bypass the pain. You **walk through it with truth.**

Here are gentle, soul-centered steps for healing through the understanding of soul contracts:

1. Replace "Why me?" with "What now?"

"Why did this happen?" pulls you into suffering.

"What now?" pulls you into purpose.(such a significant difference between the two questions and resulting feeling inside of you.)

This question does not mean you're okay with what happened. It simply shifts you into movement, evolution, and alignment with your soul path.

Try asking:

- What is this loss asking of me?
- Who am I being called to become now?
- What part of me is being awakened?

2. Honor Both Your Human Grief and Your Soul Truth

- You are a soul, yes, and you are also human. And grief is holy.
- Let yourself feel it all. Cry. Rage. Collapse. Pray. Hate God for a day if you need to. Spirit never punishes emotional honesty. **Feel everything, but don't build a home in hopelessness.**

I remember going for long walks where no other humans were around and just screaming until I was hoarse. I cried rivers of tears too. I operated on auto pilot for one year after my son's passing. The second year I felt the pain even more acutely yet differently. It was like a mind fog had lifted.

3. Speak to Your Loved One, They Can Hear You

Connection continues. Talk to them out loud. Write to them. Include them in your days. Say their name. Love doesn't disappear when a body stops breathing.

They still hear you. They still respond, through signs, feelings, dreams, music, synchronicities, and sudden peace.

I've discussed this in previous chapters. They will respond-just trust what you see/hear/smell is them.

Ask them:

- "Walk with me today."
- "Send me a sign so I know you're near."
- "Guide me. I'm listening."

4. Look for the Purpose Emerging From the Pain

Purpose does not erase grief, it gives it direction. Many soul contracts include **transformation after loss.** Sometimes your purpose is shaped because of what you've survived.

Ask:

- What needs to change now?
- Who can I help because I understand this pain?
- What truth inside me is demanding expression?

5. Transform the Love, Don't End It

Death ends a physical story, not a love story. Love must move somewhere or it collapses in on itself.

Channel it into something alive:

- A scholarship in their name
- Letters you write to them every year
- A cause they believed in
- A life lived fully, *for both of you*

This is how love becomes legacy.

6. Trust That There Is a Reunion

Every reading, every message from Spirit, every near-death experience points to one truth:

We will see each other again.

Every parent will hold their child again.

Every widow will kiss their beloved again.

Every soul finds their way home, whole, restored, loved beyond measure.

The separation is temporary. Love is eternal.

We don't come here to suffer, we come here to awaken. Loss is not here to destroy you. It is here to open you, to your soul, to your purpose, to your capacity for love, and to a truth deeper than death:

You will love again. You will feel joy again. You will see them again.

Your life did not end when theirs did, it began again.

And they are still with you. Just in a different way.

CHAPTER 8

Children and Spirit Communication

Children have a way of reminding us that the world is far more mysterious than most adults are willing to admit. They speak of things they could not possibly know. They describe loved ones who passed before they were born. They recall memories that do not belong to this lifetime or talk casually about "the man who stands by the window" when no one else is visibly there. While adults are quick to rationalize these moments, dismissing them as imagination or fantasy, children often experience genuine spiritual awareness long before they have the language or framework to understand it.

Children by nature are naturally connected to the unseen. They live nearer to the world of feeling than logic. They sense what others overlook. They trust what they feel more than what they can prove. When they are young many children speak to unseen companions, recall vivid dreams that feel more like visits than stories, and show intuitive knowing that seems impossible to explain. *(remember my story about the village in Italy?)* Rather than being unusual, these experiences may be part of the natural sensitivity that young minds possess, an unfiltered awareness that gradually fades under social conditioning.

Spirit communication through children isn't rare. It is mostly ignored. Children do not arrive in this world as blank slates. They bring a depth of awareness that extends beyond physical form, even if they cannot articulate it. Long before they are taught about the afterlife, many speak casually of "where I was before I came here," "the light I saw," or "the angel who helps me sleep." Others recount in astonishing detail events from the lives of deceased family members, people they've never seen pictures of nor have never been told about. It is far more common than most realize.

This awareness presents itself differently depending on the child. Some experience spirit visually through flashes of imagery and symbolic impressions. Others feel an unmistakable sense of someone nearby, even when they cannot see them. Some children receive information as thought-impressions, feelings, or sensations in their body. The language of spirit is subtle, and children often describe it in simple terms: "He talks without words," "She sends pictures to my head," or "I just know." *(clairaudience-hearing, clairvoyance-seeing, claircognizance-inner knowing)*

Adults often misunderstand or are afraid of their sensitivity. A child describing spirit contact might be labeled "overly imaginative," "highly emotional," "distracted," or "dramatic." Yet if they became more observant they'd often see the consistency in their descriptions and recognize an emotional tone that conveys sincerity rather than pretense.

For many children, this sensitivity begins to fade by the age of seven to nine. This is when logical thinking strengthens, social rules become internalized, and awareness shifts more fully into the physical world. They learn what is acceptable to say and what should remain unspoken. They learn that adults praise rational statements and dismiss intuitive ones. In time, they learn to hide their sensitivity even from themselves.

That does not mean their intuition disappears. It simply becomes buried beneath layers of external expectation. Some will retain their intuitive sensitivity into adolescence and adulthood, often without realizing that what they experience is something many others do not. Others may silence these abilities entirely until later in life, when a profound loss or spiritual awakening reopens the intuitive channel that has been patiently waiting beneath the surface.

Children are closer to spirit not because they are special, rather because they are still unguarded. They haven't yet built the internal walls adults carry, the defenses of disbelief, fear of judgment, or intellectual rejection of what cannot be explained. Children welcome the mysterious without needing to justify it. In that innocence lies profound wisdom, an openness that many adults spend decades trying to rediscover.

Sometimes a child will casually mention seeing a deceased relative standing near their mother, even though no photograph of that relative exists in the home. Sometimes they will reveal specific details of a grandparent's life, despite never meeting them this lifetime. Other times, children provide emotional messages from loved ones in spirit, messages carrying unmistakable truth. They do not filter. They do not embellish. They simply report what they receive.

One little boy, five years old, asked his mother why she never sang anymore. She froze. She had stopped singing years earlier after the death of her brother, who used to play guitar while she sang during family gatherings. The child had never met him. The boy continued, "The man with the guitar says you should sing again. He likes when you sing country songs best." No one had ever told this child that his uncle played guitar, let alone his favorite genre of music. The child returned to playing blocks as if nothing unusual had happened, unaware of the healing he had just delivered.

Another child experienced nighttime visits. At four years old, she began telling her father that "the lady with the blue scarf" came to see her when the lights went out. Her father was concerned. He wondered if she was having nightmares or reacting to shadows in the room. When he asked her to describe the woman, the child replied, "She has a soft voice. She smells like flowers. She tucks me in." The father went pale. His mother, who had passed years before, was soft-spoken and wore a floral perfume she never changed. The little girl had never met her.

A teenager once spoke openly about communicating with spirit but learned to stop. At thirteen, she began seeing faint flickers of light and shadow around people when they spoke, accompanied by emotional sensations she couldn't explain. When she shared this with friends, they laughed and called her strange. When she confided in a teacher, she was sent to the school counselor. Humiliated, she denied everything and shut down emotionally. Years later, she admitted that turning off her sensitivity made her feel hollow, as though she had abandoned a part of herself.

Children are often silenced not by spirit, but by the reactions of others.

Many children hesitate to speak about their experiences because they sense how adults around them might react. Even when they feel safe, they sometimes worry they will not be believed. A child who once openly spoke about members of the spirit world may suddenly avoid the subject after encountering ridicule, confusion, or emotional dismissal. They may quickly learn which topics are "allowed" and which are not. Some stop sharing altogether, not because the experiences end, simply because the emotional cost of speaking becomes too high.

Often, their silence begins with a single painful moment. A child mentions seeing someone in their room and a parent responds sharply, *"Stop making things up."* Or they describe a comforting dream of a deceased relative, and an adult cuts in with, *"That's enough. You're scaring people."* Without meaning to, adults sometimes teach children to doubt their own truth. Sensitive children who are repeatedly told that what they experience is not real may begin to disconnect from their intuition. They may become anxious about their inner world, learning to mistrust their instincts and suppress emotional expression.

Some children adapt by becoming selective with their truth. They only speak openly with people they know will listen. They might confide in a sibling versus a parent. They might draw pictures of what they feel rather than talk about it. Others hide their awareness entirely, burying it beneath logic as they grow older.

While many spiritual experiences in childhood are gentle and meaningful, some may feel overwhelming at times, especially for highly empathic children who absorb energy easily. A child who senses spirit but has no grounding may feel emotionally tired, overstimulated, or restless. They may struggle to sleep after vivid dream encounters or feel unsettled in certain places without understanding why. This is not misbehavior, it is sensitivity.

Spirit communicates with children in many ways. Some receive messages through dreams, some through emotional impressions, some through thoughts that do not feel like their own. Some children describe sensing a presence rather than seeing it. They may simply say, *"I feel like someone is here."* Others speak of seeing colors or light around people. They may not have the language for what they're experiencing, but their sincerity is unmistakable.

Lucas lost his older brother, Noah, in a tragic accident. Lucas was six at the time and seemed unusually calm during the funeral. He didn't cry or ask questions the way the adults thought he would. Several months later, Lucas began waking in the night, asking his parents if he could talk about his dreams. In these dreams, he said, Noah came to him. They would fish together at a lake, just like they had done before the accident. But one night, Lucas mentioned something new: *"Noah told me to look inside the tree."*

No one understood what he meant until Lucas walked out to the old oak in the backyard and reached into a crack in the trunk, pulling out a small metal box. Inside was a folded piece of paper with a message written by Noah years earlier: *"For my little brother someday."* Lucas had never seen the box before and had no way of knowing it existed. His mother wept as she held the note. The dream, once dismissed as a coping mechanism, delivered undeniable truth.

Another child, a four-year-old girl named Ava, spoke often of *"the angel by the window."* Her parents assumed she had created an imaginary friend. But when her mother casually asked what the angel looked like, Ava walked over to a framed photograph, pointed, and said, *"She looks like her."* The picture was of her great-grandmother Mary, who had died long before Ava was born. Ava went on to say, *"She sings to me so I know I'm safe. She wears blue when you are sad."* Her mother froze. Mary's favorite color had been blue, and Ava had never been told that. These are the moments that defy coincidence.

Not all spiritual sensitivity is dramatic. In fact, much of it is quiet. An eight-year-old boy named Jonah once told his father not to drive to school one morning because *"it didn't feel safe."* His father ignored the request until they came upon a serious highway accident that had occurred just minutes earlier. Jonah sat in silence, staring out the window. He didn't say I told you so. He didn't boast. He simply knew.

Children are often more open to spirit because they still operate from feeling rather than logic. They haven't yet learned to invalidate what they sense. They don't second-guess every impression. They don't analyze whether something is *"real"* or *"possible."* They trust instinctively. Adults could learn a great deal from such honesty.

Fear in children is often misunderstood. When a child becomes afraid after sensing spirit, adults may assume something negative or dangerous is present. But fear is not proof of danger, it's simply an emotional response to the unknown. If a child is startled by spiritual contact, it is usually because they don't understand what they're experiencing, not because something harmful is occurring. Fear dissolves when understanding begins.

A child who feels overwhelmed by spiritual impressions may ask for the light to stay on while sleeping, or may not want to be alone in a certain room. These feelings should not be dismissed or mocked. Instead, the child should be reassured: *"You are safe. You are always safe. If you feel something, talk to me about it. I will listen."* Emotional safety is the foundation of spiritual safety.

Discernment is important when supporting sensitive children to help to create clarity. There are helpful signs to look for. Genuine spiritual impressions feel calm, sincere, and emotionally grounded. They do not arrive with a need for attention or drama. The child often shares them unexpectedly, sometimes reluctantly. They carry a quiet weight of truth. In contrast, stories that shift often, grow exaggerated, or appear designed to impress others may be rooted in imagination alone. Both are valid forms of expression, but they are not the same experience.

Children who are sensitive to spirit need simple tools to feel secure. They should be taught that they always have a choice in what they experience. They can set boundaries just as they do with other parts of life. A child can say, *"I only want peaceful visitors."* They can choose, *"I don't want to feel anything while I'm sleeping."* They can say, *"That's enough for now."* Empowerment brings peace. As a parent, it's up to you to find the right words to guide your child who is in contact with spirit.

Children who grieve are especially likely to sense loved ones in spirit. Grief does not close the heart, it opens it wider. A grieving child may talk to a loved one who has passed as though that person is still present. Adults sometimes misunderstand this as denial. It is not denial at all. It is connection. A child may feel a grandmother near them, or sense a sibling who passed before birth. These experiences are not signs of confusion. They are signs of love.

Parents and caregivers do not need to understand everything about spiritual connection to support a child who experiences it. They only need to listen without judgment. Children thrive when they feel seen and heard. They shut down when they are dismissed or shamed. Supporting them is simple: believe that they are telling the truth about their own experience, even if you do not fully understand it.

Not every child with spiritual sensitivity will grow up to explore mediumship, and they shouldn't be pushed to. Sensitivity is not a career path. It is a natural awareness that may or may not develop further, depending on the choices the child makes later in life. Some children retain strong intuitive ability. Others move away from it entirely. Both paths are valid. Spiritual awareness should never be forced. It must remain free.

The role of adults is not to shape a child's spiritual experience, rather it is to make room for it. Children who are given emotional safety grow into adults who trust themselves. Children who are taught to fear or deny their inner world often struggle with self-trust later in life. It is not the experiences themselves that shape them most, it is how the adults in their lives respond.

Children remind us that life doesn't begin at logic, and it doesn't end at death. They arrive with an untamed connection to something greater, and for a short time, before the world teaches them to doubt, they speak openly of what they sense. They do not need convincing. They do not need proof. They know.

Long before a child learns about life from the world, life has already been speaking to them through spirit softly, patiently, waiting to be heard.

CHAPTER 9

Your Personal Pathway to Spirit

Building Your Own Connection

You don't need to be a trained medium to feel your loved ones in spirit. In fact, you were born with an innate ability to connect. The bond of love never dies, it merely changes form. This chapter is about helping you recognize, nurture, and trust your own personal dialogue with the unseen world.

Pause for a moment. Have you ever gotten goosebumps for no reason? Felt a sudden warmth wrap around you during a quiet moment? You might have dismissed it, but what if that was the connection? **Spirit often whispers before it speaks.**

You may already sense them in ways you haven't fully noticed, feathers left in unlikely places, a song on the radio that suddenly makes your heart swell, a dream that lingers all day long. These are not coincidences. They are invitations. Let's begin to notice them together.

Shortly after Shah's passing, he had fun turning lights off and on very often. I only felt joy when he did that. It was one of many ways of him letting me know he's always near me.

Messages in the Everyday: Signs from Spirit

Those in spirit reach out often, but gently. Their signs are subtle and filled with love, chosen specifically for you because they know what will speak to your heart.

Here are some of the most common ways spirits make contact:

Feathers:

Finding a feather in an unusual place, indoors, on your doorstep, or right after thinking of your loved one, can be a beautiful sign of their presence. One woman shared that every time she was deep in sorrow, a white feather would appear in the backseat of her locked car. No windows open. No explanation. Just a soft reminder: "You're not alone."

Coins:

Pennies, dimes, or quarters placed in your path are often used as "calling cards" by spirit. They may appear on your kitchen floor, in your shoe, or in places they simply shouldn't be. Note the date on the coin, it may hold special meaning, like a birthday or anniversary.

Have you ever bent down to pick up a coin and felt like someone was smiling over your shoulder? Pay attention. You might be collecting more than spare change.

I remember one beautiful afternoon I took my dogs and we went out for a country drive. I ended up at a lake I'd never visited before. Mine was the only car in the parking lot. The dogs and I went for a nice leisurely walk. Upon returning to my car, on the ground right outside of the driver's door, I found at least twenty pennies on the ground that hadn't been there when we arrived! I was utterly amazed and delighted! I scooped them up like the treasure they were–a sign from Shah that he had enjoyed the day with us!

Scents:

Smell is powerful. It bypasses logic and strikes the heart. The scent of pipe tobacco, a favorite perfume, or the familiar aroma of cookies baking, if these waft into your awareness with no source, it may be a loved one letting you know they're near.

One time when I was in a practice group session inside of a large conference room, we were all seated around a large oval-shaped table with our eyes closed, focused on blending with those in spirit. Suddenly I got an overwhelming scent of a roast beef dinner. I opened my eyes to see if anyone was eating. No one was. That fragrance was exactly what I smelled almost every Sunday when my mother cooked us a roast beef dinner with all the trimmings! She was there.   With me in that room. Letting me know in the best way possible of her presence.

Songs:

Music is one of the easiest and most powerful ways for spirit to communicate. That one special song might start playing in the store, on the radio, or through a shuffled playlist, right when you're thinking of them. It's not just a memory. It's a moment of connection.

My best friend left this world two months shy of her 50th birthday. We had been like two peas in a pod throughout junior and senior high school. When the band America, came out with the song "A Horse With No Name," Nancy loved it so much that her dad bought the album for her and she played it over and over and over.

Years later on a March 1st, her birthday, I was driving to Sarasota, FL thinking about Nancy and missing her. All of a sudden, the radio began playing "A Horse With No Name." I could barely see the road through the tears of joy that flowed from me.

Which song instantly brings someone to mind for you? Write it down. Spirit will often use what's already emotionally familiar to bridge the distance.

Birds and Animals:

Spirit often works through nature. A cardinal landing on your porch and staying longer than usual, a butterfly circling you, a dragonfly that hovers in your path, these creatures are sometimes used as messengers. A grieving father once shared how a bluebird began tapping on his window each morning after his daughter's passing. It continued for months, always at the same time.

A few days after the day of Shah's earthly departure, I was in our community dog park with our greyhounds. Suddenly, a hawk appeared overhead, flying very low. It continued the circular flight over my head for at least 15 minutes. I just knew it was Shah letting me know he's free now and flying high. (no, it wasn't after my dogs–they were too big for it!)

Touch, Temperature, and Tingles

Spirit doesn't always use sight or sound, **sometimes it's a feeling in your body**. A brush against your cheek. A chill down your spine. A sudden pressure on your hand or shoulder. One client shared she felt her brother squeeze her hand on the anniversary of his passing, she was completely alone, but the sensation was unmistakable.

I was sitting on the couch one time and felt a whoosh of cold air pass in front of me. Just for a second and then it was gone.

Synchronicities:

Spirit speaks through patterns, repeated numbers (like 11:11), chance encounters, or meaningful words overheard at just the right time. These are more than a coincidence. They are spiritual alignment.

What to Do When You Notice a Sign:

- **Acknowledge it.** Say "thank you" out loud or in your heart. Gratitude strengthens the connection.
- **Write it down.** Keeping a sign journal helps validate your experiences and builds trust in your awareness.
- **Stay open.** When you expect magic, you begin to see more of it.

One woman I worked with started keeping a journal of every sign she noticed. At first, she wrote only one or two things a week. But within a month, her journal filled up with entries, *"rainbow on my birthday," "his favorite song played during my walk," "her laugh in my dream."* The more she acknowledged, the more she received.

Spirits love when we acknowledge them and they'll go out of their way to give us even more to be excited about.

Dreamtime as Sacred Ground

Dreams offer a bridge between dimensions. In sleep, the logical mind softens, and the heart becomes the receiver. Your loved ones can, and do, visit during this quiet window.

These dreams feel different. They are vivid, emotional, and linger long after waking. The person in spirit may look healthy and vibrant. Their message may be simple, a hug, a smile, or a few comforting words, but it is unmistakably real.

I had another dream where Shah and I were laughing together in the kitchen. He didn't say much, just smiled and handed me a Pepsi. **That dream stayed with me for weeks.** It was simple, but so full of love, I woke up in tears, **not of sadness, but of closeness.**

Simple Tips to Invite Dream Connection:

1. **Set the Intention.** Before falling asleep, place your hand on your heart and softly say, "I'm open to receiving a visit from [name]." Speak it with sincerity and calm.

2. **Create a Calm Sleep Environment.** Dim lighting, no TV or phone distractions, and perhaps soft music can help create a receptive energy space.

3. **Place a Photo Nearby.** Setting a picture of your loved one on your nightstand is a symbolic invitation. It tells spirit you're thinking of them.

4. **Use a Dream Journal.** Keep it within reach. Upon waking, even in the middle of the night, jot down everything you remember, no matter how small. Spirit dreams can fade fast if not captured.

5. **Affirm Your Connection.** Whether or not you remember a dream, say "thank you" in the morning. Sometimes the energy of a visit is more emotional than visual.

Many people report these visits during transitional times, birthdays, anniversaries, big decisions, or moments of deep emotion. Spirit always seeks the right time and way to comfort you.

Meditation and Visualization: Opening the Channel

Quieting the mind is essential to deepening your spiritual awareness. Meditation isn't about silencing every thought, it's about becoming present enough to hear the soft voice of spirit. Visualization takes it one step further by helping you create energetic space for your loved ones to step into.

You don't have to be perfect at meditating. You only have to be willing. Even five minutes of focused breath with an open heart is enough to allow spirit to draw near.

Simple Connection Meditation:

1. **Find Stillness.** Sit in a comfortable position, feet grounded, hands relaxed. Close your eyes.

2. **Breathe Deeply.** Inhale slowly for four counts, hold for two, and exhale for six. Repeat several times.

3. **Call in Light.** Imagine a warm golden light above your head gently descending into your body, relaxing every part of you.

4. **Invite Presence.** Say internally, *"I welcome the loving presence of my [relationship to loved one]. I am open to receiving."*

5. **Feel, Don't Force.** Notice what arises, a warmth, a tingling, a subtle image or word. Trust it.

6. **Close with Gratitude.** When you're ready, thank them and gently return to the present.

With practice, this becomes easier. You may begin to sense a familiar energy around you. You may see them in your mind's eye or feel a sudden wave of calm. Spirit meets you where your heart is open. You will know it's them.

One client told me she meditates in the bathtub, candles lit, eyes closed, and her mom always "shows up" as a warmth across her shoulders. Don't overthink where or how. Let spirit meet you in the everyday.

Writing With Spirit: The Practice of Automatic Writing

Writing is a powerful tool to bridge dimensions. It allows your conscious mind to relax just enough for new insight to come forward. You don't need to be a channel or scribe, just open, honest, and willing.

How to Begin Automatic Writing:

1. **Set the Stage.** Choose a quiet space, light a candle, or play calming music if it helps.

2. **Center Yourself.** Close your eyes and take a few deep breaths. Say, "I invite [name] to communicate with me in love and truth."

3. **Start With a Question.** Write something like: "Is there anything you want me to know today?"

4. **Write Freely.** Don't censor. Let words, feelings, even fragments come through. It might feel like your own voice at first, that's okay. Keep going.

5. **Read Later.** After you've finished, step away. Come back and read what came through. Often, you'll notice phrasing or insight that didn't feel like your own.

Discerning Authentic Messages:

- Spirit communication often feels gentle, loving, and unexpectedly wise.

- There's a flow to the words, even if they seem simple.

- You may receive answers you hadn't considered.

- Spirit will never shame, frighten, or pressure you. If a message feels heavy or judgmental, pause and reset your energy.

A woman once shared that she asked her son in spirit, "What do you miss most about being here?" Through tears, she wrote the words that came: *"Hearing you laugh at your own jokes."* That answer sounded *just like him,* and she'd never have guessed it herself.

Prompts to Try:

- *"What do you see me doing that makes you proud?"*
- *"Is there something I'm overlooking right now?"*
- *"How can I feel closer to you today?"*
- *"What's your favorite memory of us?"*

This is your dialogue. There's no "right way", only your way.

If You're Still Not Sure

If you're wondering, "Am I just making this up?", you're not alone. **Doubt is a sign of sincerity.** But here's the truth: love finds a way to speak. Even if your first steps feel uncertain, trust that spirit sees your intention, and meets it with patience.

This was something I definitely grappled with in the beginning. Every time I'd silently speak to Shah in my mind, the next thought I had was him responding to me. Only I thought I was just making it up. Over time, I learned to trust that the answers I was hearing were from him. We can talk to them in the very same way we did when they were in physical form. Only this time the conversations come into our minds.

Resources for Deepening Your Connection

You don't have to walk this path alone. There are incredible communities and tools available for those seeking an authentic, personal connection with spirit.

Afterlife Institute–Self-Guided Spirit Contact

The Afterlife Research and Education Institute offers a powerful and research-supported method of making contact with departed loved ones through self-guided afterlife connection techniques. Their resources are deeply comforting and grounded in years of study.

You can explore this beautiful offering at: https://afterlifeinstitute.org/self-guided

Podcast: We Don't Die with Sandra Champlain

This heartfelt podcast shares firsthand accounts from people all over the world who've experienced visits, signs, and soul-to-soul contact with spirit. It's a rich well of encouragement and validation for those navigating loss and seeking connection.

You can listen at: https://www.wedontdie.com/

You Are the Bridge

You were never meant to live in disconnection. The soul doesn't speak in shouts, it speaks in symbols, in silence, in sudden warmth, in the breath between moments.

Spirit doesn't need a medium to reach you. You are the medium.

As you develop your intuition and trust the unseen threads weaving through your days, you'll begin to experience life with more reverence, more magic, and a deeper sense of companionship. Your loved ones are not behind you, they really do walk beside you, encouraging your steps.

Keep listening. Keep noticing. Keep asking.

And always, keep your heart open to the whispers of love that have never left.

What would your life feel like if you knew you were never alone? That's the invitation of this chapter, to move from belief to experience.

Many clients find clarity and comfort through a reading. If you feel ready to connect with someone you love, you're welcome to visit my website and see if I might be the medium for you.

CHAPTER 10

Living a Spiritually Connected Life

Transforming Your World from the Inside Out

Most people think spiritual living is about rituals, incense, and morning meditations. But what if it's really about how you answer the phone, how you pause before reacting, how you whisper "I love you" into an empty room and believe it echoes back?

What if the most profound transformation of your life didn't come from achieving something, but from remembering something? Remembering that you are never alone. That love endures beyond time. That those you have lost are still guiding you. That your connection with the spirit world is not something you seek, but something you live.

A spiritually connected life is not one separate from daily reality, it's one infused with deeper meaning, quiet trust, and sacred intention. When you live from the knowing that there is more than what your eyes can see, everything changes: your choices, your relationships, your pace, your peace.

The Shift That Changes Everything

When you know, deep in your bones, that the spirit world is real, life feels less random. There's less grasping, less fear, less need to control. That understanding doesn't eliminate pain, but it anchors you during the storms. Grief softens into purpose. Joy becomes richer. Everyday moments take on a new shimmer.

You begin to walk differently through the world. You listen more. You breathe deeper. You trust the timing of your life because you know that your soul has help, seen and unseen.

You may find yourself pausing before decisions and asking not just *what's right,* but *what feels aligned?* You might notice a gentle internal nudge, or hear your loved one's laugh in your heart, guiding you toward a choice that brings peace.

This connection can become your compass. And with it, even the hardest things, like grief, can lead to unexpected growth.

Grief as a Gateway to Grace

There was a time I believed grief would undo me. I didn't know how I could live after the death of my son. I was hollowed out. Lost. But that very loss became the fire that forged a new path.

When I chose to view grief through a spiritual lens, everything began to shift.

What does that mean, *a spiritual lens?* It means looking beyond the surface pain and asking deeper questions:

- *What is my soul learning through this?*
- *How might this shape me into someone more open-hearted, more present, more compassionate?*
- *Where is the invitation in the sorrow?*

This perspective doesn't bypass the ache. It honors it. But it also asks you to lean into the belief that love endures, that your person still exists, and that the pain you feel is not the end of the story. In fact, it may be the beginning of something new.

Through loss, I became who I am today. A woman who communicates with spirit. Who helps others feel whole again. Who knows in her soul that the veils are thin, and that healing is always possible.

Grief cracked me open. But it didn't destroy me. It awakened me. And it can do the same for you.

Creating a Life that Includes Those in Spirit

Living spiritually connected means you continue your relationship with your loved ones, not as a past, but as a presence.

You can do this by building rituals, spaces, and traditions that honor the bond you still share.

Think of spirit like an old friend who texts you memes at exactly the right moment. They're not just wise, they're witty. They know what you need: sometimes a sign, sometimes a song, sometimes a reason to smile in the cereal aisle.

Personal Rituals and Sacred Space

Designating a small area of your home as a sacred corner can be both comforting and empowering. Include a candle, a photo, a small token or belonging, and perhaps a journal or letter. This becomes your quiet place for reflection, connection, and conversation.

Light the candle when you want to speak to them. Place fresh flowers there on important days. Let it be a visual reminder that love lives on.

Annual Celebrations and Legacy Days

One of the most beautiful examples I know is a couple who lost their son twenty-six years ago. Every year on the anniversary of his passing, they meet with his closest friends at his favorite Mexican restaurant. They share stories, laughter, and memories. It's not a sad occasion, it's a living tribute.

You might:

- Host an *Angelversary Gathering* with music, favorite foods, and shared stories

- Spend a *Tribute Day* doing things they loved, fishing, gardening, crafting
- Create a digital memory book with photos and anecdotes from friends and family
- Sponsor a charitable act in their name each year

These are not acts of grief. They are acts of devotion. They say, *"You mattered. You still do. I love you so much."*

Standing Strong in What You Know

When you begin living in alignment with spirit, not everyone will understand. Some may question you. Others may withdraw. Even those closest to you may challenge your beliefs.

You are not alone in this.

The point is not to convince anyone else. The point is to trust your own knowing.

When doubt creeps in, whether internal or external, ask yourself:

- *What have I experienced that no one can take from me?*
- *What brings me comfort, peace, and expansion?*
- *Does my belief harm anyone, or does it bring healing?*

Your truth is enough. You do not owe anyone an explanation for what so clearly speaks to your soul. Stand in that.

Daily Practices for Spirit-Led Living

To deepen your spiritual connection in everyday life, consider incorporating small but meaningful practices:

- **Morning Alignment:** Begin each day with a quiet question: "Spirit, how can I serve today? Who needs my light?" Listen for the answer in your heart.

- **Soul Check-ins:** Pause throughout the day to place your hand over your heart and breathe. Ask: "Am I present? Am I acting with love?"

- **Evening Gratitude:** Each night, speak or write three ways spirit showed up in your day, through signs, synchronicities, or unexpected kindness.

These small acts become your rhythm, gently anchoring you in the truth that you are always supported.

What If I Don't Get a Sign?

It's one of the most tender questions I hear: *"Why haven't I received a sign?"*

If you've been quietly hoping, watching the clock for repeated numbers, scanning the sky for a feather, dreaming of a message, but nothing seems to come, know this:

You are not doing anything wrong. You are not blocked. You are not less connected than someone else.

Sometimes, in our longing, we become so focused on one type of sign that we miss the subtle ones already unfolding around us, a feeling in your chest when you think of them, a song that plays at just the right time, a quiet knowing that arrives without explanation.

Spirit doesn't always speak through drama. Sometimes they whisper.

And sometimes, they wait until you're in the right space, quiet, open, soft enough to notice.

Keep talking to them. Keep inviting them in. Then gently, lovingly, let go of expectation. That release becomes an opening. (Note: Expectations are like giving someone a demand. That doesn't work in real life nor in the spirit world.)

Trust this: They are there. And they will reach you in the way that is best for you.

Your only job is to stay open, stay curious, and know that true love is never silent.

Reflection Questions & Journaling Prompts

Use these to deepen your understanding and connection:

- *When do I feel most connected to spirit? What am I doing in those moments?*
- *What fears or doubts come up for me around spiritual beliefs, and where do they come from?*
- *How has my grief changed me, for better or worse?*
- *What new traditions or rituals can I use to keep my loved one's memory alive?*
- *What do I want others to remember about how I choose to love beyond death?*

I know another gentleman who writes a letter to his eternal son in the present tense. He talks about the sports team they both love and how well or poorly they're doing. He let his son know how his health is these days. He speaks with him as though he's still here and, of course; he is! This brings the gentlemen comfort and pleasure and keeps the conversation going.

For those of you old enough to remember, think of The Invisible Man! We couldn't see him, yet we knew he was always there and could hold a conversation too!

Walking This Path With Intention

To live a spiritually connected life is to live awake. It's seeing meaning in the mundane. To speak to your loved ones as if they hear you, because they do. It's walking through your grief as a student of the soul, not as a victim of circumstance.

You are not just surviving loss. You are allowing it to shape you. To open you. To teach you to live more fully.

Spirit is not far. It's just quieter than the world. And when you listen with your heart, you'll hear them everywhere, in laughter, in music, in dreams, in sunlight, in the breeze.

They are not gone. They are walking this path with you.

Keep going. You're doing beautifully.

As you step into each new day, carry with you the certain knowing that love, your deepest emotion, knows no boundaries. That your grief, tender though it is, has opened you to grace, connection, and purpose. You are not merely surviving loss, you are embodying love's eternal promise in every breath, decision, and gentle pause. Let this be your invitation to live a life held, inspired, and led by spirit. And may you always feel the quiet, faithful presence beside you, walk on, dear one.

Thank you for allowing me to walk this path with you. If my words have resonated, and you'd like to connect more deeply, I offer private sessions and share more tools for healing and growth at www.aperfectsoul.com.

Quick Reference Guide:

Tools for Spirit Connection

Simple Connection Meditation

1. Sit quietly with your feet on the floor.
2. Place your hand over your heart.
3. Close your eyes and breathe gently.
4. Say aloud or silently: "Spirit, I invite your presence now."
5. Notice any shift, sensations, thoughts, emotions.
6. End by saying "Thank you," whether or not you felt anything specific.

Automatic Writing Steps

1. Begin with a grounding breath or short meditation.
2. Write a question at the top of your journal page.
3. Write without judgment or editing, let the words flow.
4. If unsure, write: "What do you want me to know?" and wait.
5. Close by writing "Thank you" and rereading with an open heart.

Signs from Spirit Checklist

☐ Songs or lyrics at meaningful moments

☐ Repeating numbers (111, 444, etc.)

☐ Dreams that feel "different"

☐ Scents or sensations with no physical source

☐ Random memories that bring sudden comfort

☐ Objects found in unusual places (coins, feathers, photos)

Daily Anchors

- Morning: Set an intention.
- Midday: Hand over heart, "Am I present?"
- Evening: Gratitude for 3 signs or moments of beauty.

Resources for Grief Support

Compassionate Friends (support for parents who've lost a child(ren)—https://www.compassionatefriends.org/

GriefShare (peer-support groups, online and in-person)—https://www.griefshare.org/

The Dougy Center (services for grieving children & families)—https://www.dougy.org/

Modern Loss—online community and real-world support https://modernloss.com/tag/support-groups/

Open to Hope—grief resources, articles, and videos—https://www.opentohope.com/

What's Your Grief—grief education, courses, blog.—https://whatsyourgrief.com/

TAPS (Tragedy Assistance Program for Survivors)—peer support for military loss— https://www.taps.org/

American Widow Project—community and healing for military widows— https://americanwidowproject.org/

The Dinner Party—peer-support potlucks for young adults navigating grief— https://www.thedinnerparty.org

Online Grief Communities like Grieving.com, Grief in Common, Hope Again, Grief Healing

SAMHSA—for broader mental health and grief resources, especially in crisis— https://www.samhsa.gov

Recommended Books

- *"Signs: The Secret Language of the Universe,"* by Laura Lynne Jackson
- *"The Afterlife of Billy Fingers,"* by Annie Kagan
- *"It's OK That You're Not OK,"* by Megan Devine
- *"Hello from Heaven,"* by Bill & Judy Guggenheim
- *"Grief Day by Day,"* by Jan Warner

Podcasts

- We Don't Die–personal accounts of afterlife experiences
- Grief Out Loud–honest stories of loss
- Terrible, Thanks for Asking–raw and real conversations about grief

Glossary of Spiritual Terms

After-death communication (ADC)

Spontaneous or intentional experiences where people sense, see, hear, or feel the presence of a loved one who has passed away.

Angelversary

The anniversary of a loved one's passing, often remembered with love, rituals, or celebration.

Apport

An object that appears mysteriously during a séance or spiritual experience, believed to be moved or created by a spirit.

Automatic writing

Writing that comes through without conscious thought, believed to be guided by a spirit or higher self.

Clairs

The different ways mediums receive information from the spirit world. These include several types of 'clear' senses.

Clairvoyance

The ability to see images or visions in the mind's eye, such as people, objects, or scenes from a spirit communicator.

Clairaudience

The ability to hear messages from spirit internally, such as names, phrases, or music.

Clairsentience

The ability to feel emotions, physical sensations, or energy from spirit.

Claircognizance

The ability to simply know information without being told, as if the answer appears in the mind.

Clairalience

The ability to smell scents that are connected to someone in spirit, like perfume or smoke.

Clairgustance

The ability to taste something associated with a person in spirit, such as a favorite food or drink.

Energy field

The invisible layer of energy around a person, sometimes called an aura, which holds emotional and spiritual information.

Evidential mediumship

A form of mediumship that focuses on providing clear, specific details from spirit to prove their identity.

Grounding

A technique to connect your body and energy to the earth to feel stable and balanced, especially after spiritual work.

Mental mediumship

Receiving messages from spirit through the mind, like seeing images, hearing words, or sensing feelings internally.

Physical mediumship

Spirit communication that creates visible or audible effects in the physical environment, like moving objects or direct voices.

Psychic vs. Medium

A psychic reads your personal energy; a medium connects with loved ones in spirit. All mediums are psychic, but not all psychics are mediums.

Spirit guide

A spiritual helper or teacher who supports you from the spirit world, often working with you through life.

Spirit world

The non-physical realm where souls go after death; believed to be a place of love, peace, and growth.

Sitter

The person receiving a reading from a medium, the one seeking to connect with a loved one in spirit.

Soul contract

An agreement made by a soul before birth to experience certain events, relationships, or lessons in this life.

Synchronicity

Meaningful coincidences that seem too perfect to be random, often seen as signs or guidance from spirit.

Validation

Clear, specific evidence that confirms the identity or message of a spirit loved one during a reading.

Veil

A metaphor for the boundary between the physical world and the spirit world. Mediums are said to lift or peer through this veil.

Vibration

The energetic frequency of a person or spirit. Higher vibrations are linked to love, peace, and spiritual connection.

Visitation dream

A special kind of dream where a loved one in spirit appears vividly and leaves a lasting emotional impression.

About the Author

Sharon Valenti is an evidential medium whose work is rooted in compassion, integrity, and a deep respect for the ongoing life of the soul. Her path into mediumship began after the heartbreaking loss of her son, Shah. In the quiet moments of grief, unexpected signs and subtle moments of connection awakened Sharon to a truth she could no longer ignore — that love continues, consciousness survives, and the bonds we share do not end with physical death.

Driven by a need to understand these experiences and honor her connection with Shah, Sharon sought formal training with respected teachers, including Heather Scavetta, John Holland, and Tony Stockwell. Her development later led her to London's renowned Arthur Findlay College, where she continued refining her sensitivity, her evidential clarity, and her commitment to ethical mediumship.

Sharon's work is shaped by both her personal healing and her desire to help others find their own. Whether she is bringing through a loved one in spirit, guiding a sitter through their grief, or demystifying mediumship for readers, she approaches every encounter with warmth, humility, and a sincere wish to offer comfort and truth.

www.ingramcontent.com/pod-product-compliance
Lightning Source LLC
Chambersburg PA
CBHW021204130626
46554CB00005B/1987